北大版对外汉语教材·短期培训系列·组合汉语

48小时汉语速成
基础篇

Learn Chinese in 48 Hours
—A Crash Course of Elementary Chinese

课 本
TEXTBOOK

下 册
Volume Two

编 著　吕必松
英文审订　鲁健骥
英文翻译　赵萍萍
　　　　　袁　媛

北京大学出版社
PEKING UNIVERSITY PRESS

图书在版编目(CIP)数据

48小时汉语速成.基础篇(下册)/吕必松编著.—北京:北京大学出版社,2010.7
(北大版对外汉语教材·短期培训系列·组合汉语)
ISBN 978-7-301-17240-7

Ⅰ.48… Ⅱ.吕… Ⅲ.①汉语-对外汉语教学-教材 Ⅳ.H195.4

中国版本图书馆CIP数据核字(2010)第098826号

书　　　名:48小时汉语速成·基础篇(下册)
著作责任者:吕必松　编著
责 任 编 辑:沈　岚
标 准 书 号:ISBN 978-7-301-17240-7/H·2511
出 版 发 行:北京大学出版社
地　　　址:北京市海淀区成府路205号　100871
网　　　址:http://www.pup.cn
电　　　话:邮购部 62752015　发行部 62750672　编辑部 62752028　出版部 62754962
电 子 邮 箱:zpup@pup.pku.edu.cn
印　刷　者:北京大学印刷厂
经　销　者:新华书店
　　　　　　787毫米×1092毫米　16开本　16.25印张　400千字
　　　　　　2010年7月第1版　2010年7月第1次印刷
印　　　数:1—3000册
定　　　价:60.00元(全二册)(含1张MP3)

未经许可,不得以任何方式复制或抄袭本书之部分或全部内容。
版权所有,侵权必究　　举报电话:010-62752024
　　　　　　　　　　　电子邮箱:fd@pup.pku.edu.cn

目 录

Contents

使用说明 ·· 1
How to use this book

第十六课　马先生在家吗? ··· 1
Lesson Sixteen　Is Mr.Ma at Home?
1. 汉字的造字方法(1)：象形字/5
   Ways of formation of *Hanzi* (1)：the pictographic *zi*
2. 字义例解和部件释义/5
   Explanation of the meanings of *Hanzi* and *Hanzi* components
   纟 气 手 扌 辶 以 话
3. 字词用法例解/6
   Explanation of the usages of *zi* and *zi*-groups
   (1) 他还没回来呢
   (2) 你打他的手机吧
   (3) 他的手机号码是 13301010788

第十七课　请你替我向她问好 ·· 7
Lesson Seventeen　Please Say Hello to Her
1. 汉字的造字方法(2)：指事字 /11
   Ways of formation of *Hanzi* (2)：the indicative *zi*
2. 字义例解和部件释义/12
   Explanation of the meanings of *Hanzi* and *Hanzi* components
   车 火 白 饣 饭 问
3. 字词用法例解/13
   Explanation of the usages of *zi* and *zi*-groups
   (1) 好久不见了
   (2) 是吗
   (3) 太好了

1

第十八课　我想请你吃午饭 …………………………………………………… 14
Lesson Eighteen　I Would Like to Invite You to Lunch
1. 汉字的造字方法(3)：会意字/18

   Ways of formation of *Hanzi* (3)：the ideographic *zi*
2. 字义例解和部件释义/19

   Explanation of the meanings of *Hanzi* and *Hanzi* components

   比　灬　点　店　矢　知　道
3. 字词用法例解/20

   Explanation of the usages of *zi* and *zi*-groups

   好像……

第十九课　北京饭店在哪儿？ …………………………………………………… 21
Lesson Nineteen　Where is Beijing Hotel?
1. 汉字的造字方法(4)：形声字/26

   Ways of formation of *Hanzi* (4)：the pictophonetic *zi*
2. 字义例解和部件释义/27

   Explanation of the meanings of *Hanzi* and *Hanzi* components

   面　东　多　从　分　立　站　钟　阝
3. 字词用法例解/28

   Explanation of the usages of *zi* and *zi*-groups

   (1) 请问

   (2) 就到

第二十课　复习(四) …………………………………………………… 29
Lesson Twenty　Review (4)

第二十一课　你们喝什么饮料？ …………………………………………………… 35
Lesson Twenty-one　What Kind of Drinks Would You Like?
1. 词的组合生成/39

   The combination of *zi*-groups
2. 字义例解和部件释义/40

   Explanation of the meanings of *Hanzi* and *Hanzi* components

   米　艹　菜　井　欠　饮　欢　酉
3. 字词用法例解/41

   Explanation of the usages of *zi* and *zi*-groups

   呢

第二十二课 你们想吃什么菜？ ……………………………………………… **42**
Lesson Twenty-two　What Kind of Dish Would You Like?

1. 词法结构(1)：限定结构/46

    Zi-group structures (1)：the restrictive structure

2. 字义例解和部件释义/47

    Explanation of the meanings of *Hanzi* and *Hanzi* components

    亻　清　烤　鸟　鸡　鸭　鱼　鲤

3. 字词用法例解/48

    Explanation of the usages of *zi* and *zi*-groups

    (1) 吧

    (2) 好的

    (3) 红烧的

第二十三课 你们要什么主食？ ……………………………………………… **49**
Lesson Twenty-three　What Staple Food Would You Like?

1. 词法结构(2)：动受结构/53

    Zi-group structures (2)：the action-recipient structure

2. 字义例解和部件释义/54

    Explanation of the meanings of *Hanzi* and *Hanzi* components

    勹　包　石　碗　饺　饱　𤣩　现

3. 字词用法例解/55

    Explanation of the usages of *zi* and *zi*-groups

    (1) 动字重叠

    (2) "南方"和"北方"

    (3) 名字用作量字

第二十四课 共计九百零二元 ……………………………………………… **57**
Lesson Twenty-four　Altogether 902 Yuan

1. 词法结构(3)：表示动作结果的动补结构/61

    Zi-group structures (3)：the action-complement structure
    showing the result of an action

2. 字义例解和部件释义/63

    Explanation of the meanings of *Hanzi* and *Hanzi* components

    戈　夂　少　千　钱　优　彳

3. 字词用法例解/64

    Explanation of the usages of *zi* and *zi*-groups

    (1) 货币单位

    (2) 下次、下回

第二十五课　复习（五） ……………………………………………… 65
Lesson Twenty-five　Review (5)

第二十六课　马总正在开会 ……………………………………… 69
Lesson Twenty-six　General Manager Ma is at a Meeting

1. 句法结构(1)：主体和述体/74

   Sentence structure(1): the topic and the comment
2. 字义例解和部件释义/75

   Explanation of the meanings of *Hanzi* and *Hanzi* components

   ⺮　等　开　页　顺　预　约　男
3. 字词用法例解/77

   Explanation of the usages of *zi* and *zi*-groups

   (1) 正在

   (2) "老……"和"小……"

第二十七课　让您久等了 ………………………………………… 79
Lesson Twenty-seven　Sorry for Having Kept You Waiting So Long

1. 句法结构(2)：基本句的组合生成/83

   Sentence structure (2): formation of basic sentences
2. 字义例解和部件释义/84

   Explanation of the meanings of *Hanzi* and *Hanzi* components

   贝　目　牛　合
3. 字词用法例解/85

   Explanation of the usages of *zi* and *zi*-groups

   "的"字结构

第二十八课　这是互利双赢的好项目 ……………………………… 86
Lesson Twenty-eight　This is a Mutually Beneficial Win-win Project

1. 句法结构(3)：复合句的组合生成/91

   Sentence structure (3): formation of compound sentences
2. 字义例解和部件释义/92

   Explanation of the meanings of *Hanzi* and *Hanzi* components

   巾　市　衤　礻　补　利　力　艹　算　定
3. 字词用法例解/93

   Explanation of the usages of *zi* and *zi*-groups

   (1) 夫人

   (2) 他会来的

目录

第二十九课　贵客到了 …………………………………………… 95
Lesson Twenty-nine　The Distinguished Guest is Arriving
1. 句法结构(4)：复杂句的组合生成/101
   Sentence structure (4)：combination of complex sentences
2. 字义例解和部件释义/101
   Explanation of the meanings of *Hanzi* and *Hanzi* components
   彡　耳　由　加　土
3. 字词用法例解/102
   Explanation of the usages of *zi* and *zi*-groups
   是的

第三十课　复习(六) …………………………………………… 103
Lesson Thirty　Review(6)

附录1　汉语音节的语音结构和书写方法 ……………………… 109
Appendix 1　Phonetic structures and spelling rules of Chinese syllables

附录2　字词表 …………………………………………………… 116
Appendix 2　Table of *zi* and *zi*-groups

附录3　"唱读和口译"答案 ……………………………………… 148
Appendix 3　Key to *Read aloud and interpret*

使用说明

本书是根据"组合汉语"理论编写的速成汉语教材,是《组合汉语系列》教材的组成部分。《组合汉语系列》教材的编写宗旨是尽可能反映汉语和汉语学习的特点,使汉语和汉字易教易学,让学生用最少的时间学到最需要的汉语。

本教材的教学对象是会英语的成年汉语初学者。

本教材共计30课,分上、下两册,每册15课。每五课为一个单元,逢五、逢十的是复习课。教学内容包括391个汉字和由这些汉字组成的673个词语(另有203个补充词语),以及由这些汉字和词语组成的108个句型和22课课文。课文都是以话题为中心的会话。学会了这些内容,在中国生活和工作就可以用汉语进行一般性交际。这些内容也是进一步学好汉语的坚实基础,在此基础上,学习汉语的速度将会加快。

本教材预计教学时间为60课时(按每课时45～50分钟计算,约合48小时),平均每课2课时。要求学生用与上课大致相等的时间进行预习和复习,如果没有时间预习和复习,教学进度要适当放慢。

本教材每课的教学内容和课堂教学要求如下:

1. 笔画(1～9课)。列出当课所教汉字中包含的新笔画,要求学生学会识别这些笔画,通过唱读、黑板临写等方式记住它们的名称和掌握书写方法。

2. 部件(11～29课)。列出当课所教汉字中的部分常用部件,要求学生学会识别这些部件,掌握它们的结构特点,理解它们的意思(有些部件只是书写符号,不代表任何意思),通过唱读、黑板临写等方式记住它们的名称和在汉字中的位置,并掌握书写方法。

3. 生字和生词。列出当课课文中出现的生字以及由当课和以前学过的汉字组合生成的生词,要求学生朗读这些字词,并记住它们的读音和意思。字词的英文翻译是为了帮助学生理解相应字词的意思,但是学生必须了解,两种语言字词的意思和用法不是完全对等的,汉语字词的确切意思和用法要在句子和课文中体会和把握。

4. 补充生词。补充生词不要求学生记住,以后如在课文中出现,还要作为生词重新列出。补充生词中的汉字都是学过的,所以容易记忆,教师如果补充练习内容,也可在补充的练习中适当使用。

本教材主张直接教授汉字的读音,汉字(以及部分词语)后面的括弧里标注的汉语拼音主要供教师参考,不必要求学生认读。学生在字词的读音上如果出现偏误,偏误主要表现在声母、韵母和声调这三个方面,教师可以根据发音原理有针对性地加以纠正,也不必借助于汉语拼音。

5. 句子理解(3～14课)。列出当课课文中出现的新句型,通过字、词对译和整句翻译两种办法帮助学生理解汉语字词的意思、句子的结构特点以及与英语的区别。希望学生能从中体会到汉语的一种结构形式所表示的意思相当于英语的什么结构形式所表示的意思,英语的一个意思用汉语怎样表达。这项内容主要供学生自学,教师不必逐句讲解,但是要提醒学生课前预习,并准备解答学生可能提出的疑难问题。

6. 会话(从第三课开始)。会话就是以话题为中心的课文。各课会话都设定真实的情境,会话内容符合在日常生活和工作中进行人际交往的实际需要,用于会话的语句都是最常用的标准普通话。采用以话题为中心的会话体课文,是为了帮助初学者学会用汉语交际。这项教学内容要通过扮演角色等方式进行反复操练。

7. 替换练习。设置替换练习的目的是帮助学生掌握汉语句型,同时通过适量的课堂操练帮助学生复习、巩固当课和以前各课学过的字、词、句,尽可能达到准确、流利。如果觉得分量太大,教师可以有选择地组织操练,不必求全。

8. 汉字唱读和空写(1～14课)。"唱读"是指全班跟着教师大声齐读,"空写"就是大家跟着教师用手指凌空书写。这项内容的教学目的是帮助学生记住汉字笔画的名称,熟练掌握汉字的书写方法。大声齐唱齐写,边唱边写,可以让学生放松,形成轻松愉快的课堂气氛。

本教材归纳的汉字笔画共计28个,其中基本笔画(书写时笔向基本不变的笔画)6个,复合笔画(书写时笔向改变一次的笔画)9个,复杂笔画(书写时笔向改变两次以上的笔画)13个。(见本书附录1《汉字笔画表》)学会了这28个笔画,就是学会了汉字的全部笔画。这28个笔画只有8个概念(横、竖、撇、捺、点、提、弯、钩),这8个概念既是笔画的名称,也是笔画形状和笔画书写方法的名称。我们相信,通过前14课的练习,学生完全可以记住这些笔画的名称,同时掌握汉字的结构特点和书写方法。

9. 语音练习和汉语拼音教学(1～19课)。本教材把声调作为语音教学的重点,同时注意突出第二语言学习者普遍的语音难点。组合汉语主张直接用汉字教学发音和说话,在学生学会汉语拼音之前(即第十九课之前),不必要求他们认读汉字(以及部分词语)后面所注的汉语拼音。学生在字词的读音上如果出现偏误,偏误主要表现在声母、韵母和声调这三个方面,教师可以根据发音原理有针对性地加以纠正。本教材也重视汉语拼音教学,从第六课开始,陆续用汉语拼音教学声母和韵母,从第十一课开始,陆续教学音节识读。(前五课的语音练习主要是声调练习)所教声母、韵母和音节的汉语拼音都是学生已经学过的汉字中所包含的,所以实践上是用汉字的读音教学汉语拼音,而不是用汉语拼音教学汉字的读音。至第十九课,已基本教完《汉语拼音方案》的相关内容,以后就可以指导学生借助于汉语拼音学习汉字的读音。采用这样的办法,不但可以减少汉语拼音对正确发音的误导,而且可以强化对汉字的感知。

10. 汉语知识。本教材的汉语知识包括语音知识、汉字知识、语法知识和交际知识等,这些内容主要供学生预习和复习(最好要求预习),教师可以结合字、词、句的教学适当加以提示,不必逐项专门讲解。其中的"字义例解和部件释义"是为了帮助学生理解和记忆汉字,教学内容从当课出现的汉字中选择,不求全面、系统。学生不必深究每一个汉字的造字方法和每一个部件的意思。

本教材尽可能少用语言学上的专业术语,大部分语法项目都放在词汇层面上处理,只对少数语法难点进行专项解释,解释力求简明。对语法的掌握要靠语感,语法解释只能起辅助作用。

本教材所说的"词"是"字组"的意思,不包括单音节"词"。我们也不使用"语素"的概念。其他语法书上所说的单音节词和语素在本教材中都叫"字"。

11. 根据组合汉语理论,本教材的基本教学方法是以"字"为基本单位的"组合生成",即:由笔画、部件组合生成汉字,由汉字组合生成词语,由汉字、词语组合生成句子。字、词、句的组合生成都遵循"1+1=1"(合二为一)的普遍规则。"组合"实际上是意义的组合,意思相关的字词才能互相组合。因此,教学中要突出词语和句子的语义结构。词语的语义结构包括限定(饭店,红茶,很好)、动受(吃饭,看书)、述补(看见,说得好,高一点儿)、并列(身体,喜欢)、主述(身体好,经济落后)等,句子的语义结构主要是主体和述体之间的语义关系。主体代表谁或什么,是已知信息和述体陈述的对象;述体说明主体做什么或怎么样,是使知信息并用于陈述主体。"谁(什么)——做什么(怎么样)"是汉语基本句的固定格式。语义结构教学不是靠理论讲解,而是靠对实例的适当提示让学生体会和理解。

12. 本教材有《练习册》和《教学指南》相配套。课外练习侧重于读和写,主要内容包括笔画和部件的记忆、汉字的书写、阅读理解和造句、写话等。课堂教学则要侧重于听和说的练习。《教学指南》具有教案的特点,如果作为教案使用,可以更好地把握组合汉语教学的基本程序和方法,也可以节省备课时间。

编者

How to use this book

This textbook is compiled for adult English speakers to learn Chinese based on the theory of "Combinative Chinese". It's a crash course of Chinese and a volume of the "Combinative Chinese Series" which is to try to reflect the characteristics of the Chinese language, in an attempt to make both teaching and learning easy, and enable learners to acquire the most needed Chinese within the least time.

There are 30 lessons divided into two volumes each with 15 lessons. The textbook includes 391 *Hanzi* and 673 *zi*-groups and 203 additional *zi*-groups, and these are used in 108 sentence patterns and 22 texts. All the texts are dialogues focused on topics. By mastering all of these contents, learners will be able to carry out general communications in Chinese when they stay and work in China, meanwhile they have a solid foundation for further and faster learning.

It is planned that it takes 60 class hours (45～50 minutes for a class, about 48 hours in all) to complete this course, 2 class hours each lesson. Learners are required to use approximately the same time to prepare and review the lesson, if no time for preview and review, the progress of teaching should be slowed.

The contents to be taught and classroom requirements are as follows:

1. *Hanzi* strokes (Lesson 1～9). This section lists new strokes of *Hanzi* in the lesson. Learners are required to know how to recognize and write them and remember their names by reading aloud, copying them on the blackboard, etc.

2. *Hanzi* components (Lesson 11～29). This section lists some commonly used *Hanzi* components. Learners are required to recognize them, grasp their structures and understand their meanings (some *Hanzi* components are just written symbols that do not bear any meaning). By reading them aloud, copying them on the blackboard, etc, the learners should memorize their names, their positions in different *Hanzi* and master the ways to write them.

3. *Zi* and *zi*-groups. Attached to each lesson is a list of new *Hanzi* appearing in it and the new *zi*-groups composed of the *Hanzi* in the lessons. Learners are supposed to read them aloud and learn their pronunciations and meanings by heart. The English equivalents given to the *zi* and *zi*-groups are just to help learners know their meanings. Learners must be aware that their meanings and usages are not always

How to use this book

equal to their English counterparts and their meanings and usages can be grasped exactly only by understanding the sentences and texts.

4. Additional *zi*-groups. These are not required to be remembered and will be listed as new ones when they appear in the next lessons. The additional *zi*-groups are easy to learn because they are composed of *Hanzi* that have been learned. It is suggested that the teacher should use them when giving extra exercises.

Teachers are encouraged to teach learners to read *Hanzi* without referring to the *pinyin* transcriptions, though they are provided in the brackets for teachers' reference. In case a *Hanzi* or *zi*-group is incorrectly read, i.e. the initial, final or tone is mispronounced, the teacher just corrects it according to the method of articulation without referring to the *pinyin* transcription.

5. Sentence comprehension (Lesson 3～14). New sentence patterns in each lesson are listed and the meanings of *zi* and *zi*-groups, structural features of sentences and differences from the similar English patterns are explained in two ways: 1) transliterating the *zi* and *zi*-groups in them one by one; 2) translating the whole sentence. Students should know how a structure form in Chinese is expressed in English and how a certain English meaning is expressed in Chinese. This part is mainly for students to learn by themselves. Teachers do not have to explain them sentence by sentence in class, but they may advice the learners do some preview and teachers are ready to answer their questions.

6. Dialogues (from Lesson 3 on). Dialogues are texts on various topics. The dialogues in each lesson, based on authentic situations, meet the needs for communications in daily life and work. The sentences in the dialogues are most commonly used in standard Chinese. The topical dialogues are helpful for learners, they can use them immediately. We suggest they practise the dialogues by playing different roles.

7. Substitution drills. The aim of substitution drills is to help learners grasp Chinese sentence patterns, and at the same time review and consolidate the *Hanzi*, *zi*-groups and sentences they learn in the lessons through exercises. Students should master this section as correctly and fluently as possible. Teachers can choose some of the drills for the students under time pressure.

8. Reading aloud and "finger writing" the *Hanzi* (Lesson 1～14). Reading aloud means that the students follow the teacher to read aloud *Hanzi*. "Finger writing" means the students follow the teacher to write *Hanzi* with their forefingers. This section is to help the learners memorize the names of *Hanzi* strokes, and master the ways to write them. Those exercises will help to create an easy-going classroom atmosphere in which

the students can study in a relaxed manner.

In this book, 28 strokes are introduced among which 6 are basic strokes (those that the pen moves nearly in one direction in writing), 9 compound strokes (those that the pen moves with one turn), and 13 complex strokes (those that the pen moves with two or more turns). (See Appendix: "Table of the *Hanzi* Strokes") If you have learned these 28 strokes, you will have mastered all the *Hanzi* strokes in 8 notions (horizontal, vertical, left-falling, right-falling, dot, rising, bending, hook). They are not only the names of strokes, but also the shapes and the ways of writing them. We believe through the exercises in the previous fourteen lessons, learners will be able to learn them all and master their structural characteristics.

9. Pronunciation drills and *Hanyu Pinyin* teaching (Lessons 1~19). This textbook is focused on tone in pronunciation teaching and at the same time highlights the universal phonetic speech difficulties. According to Combinative Chinese, *Hanzi* are directly used to teach pronunciation and speaking. *Hanzi* (and some *zi*-groups), followed by the *Hanyu Pinyin*, are not required to recognize and read before learners grasp *Hanyu Pinyin* (namely before Lesson 19). Learners' *Pinyin* problems on *Zi* or *zi*-groups mainly exist in the consonants, vowels or tones. Teachers can be well targeted to correct them according to pronunciation principles. This textbook is also attached importance to *Pinyin* teaching, consonants and vowels teachings beginning from Lesson 6, and syllables from Lesson 11. (The former five lessons are focused on tone practice) all taught consonants, vowels and syllables in *Hanyu Pinyin* are included in the *Hanzi* that learners have learned, so *Hanyu Pinyin* is taught through *Hanzi*'s pronunciation, instead of *Hanzi*'s pronunciation through *Hanyu Pinyin*. To Lesson 19 the Chinese Phonetic Alphabet is nearly completed. Then the learners can be guided to learn *Hanzi* by means of *Pinyin*. This approach can not only reduce the wrong pronunciation misled by *Pinyin*, but also strengthen the perception of *Hanzi*.

10. Chinese Language ABC. This section includes knowledge of Chinese phonetics, *Hanzi*, grammar and communication. It is mainly provided for the learners to preview, which is required, and review the lessons. Teachers can give certain tips when teaching *Hanzi*, *zi*-groups and sentences. The section "explanation of the meanings of *Hanzi* and *Hanzi* components" is to help students understand and memorize *Hanzi*. The teaching contents of this section are chosen from *Hanzi* in the lesson concerned, but not a comprehensive and systematic treatise of *Hanzi* and components. Learners do not have to understand the formation of each *Hanzi* and meaning of each *Hanzi* components.

In this textbook we try to use as less linguistic terms as possible. Most grammar

How to use this book

items are dealt with in vocabulary teaching. Specific explanations are just limited to a few difficult items. The explanations are done as concisely as possible. The mastering of grammar relies on the *instinctive* feel for the language. Explanation only plays the role of an aid in language teaching.

"Cí"(词) in this textbook means *zi*-group in which the single syllabic "word"is not included, and the term "morpheme"is not used. The so-called single syllable "word" and morphemes in other grammar books are called "*zi*" in this textbook.

11. According to the theory of "Combinative Chinese", the main teaching method in this textbook can be summarized as "combination and formation" with "*zi*" as the basic unit. By "combination and formation", we mean this: *zi* is formed by the combination of strokes and *zi* components, the *zi*-group is formed by the combination of *zi* and the sentence is composed of *zi* and *zi*-groups. The combination of *zi*, *zi*-groups and sentences all follow the universal rule of "$1+1=1$"(two combined into one). Actually combination means the combination of meanings, i.e. the *zi* and *zi*-groups can be combined only when they are relevant to each other in meaning. Therefore the semantic structures of *zi*-groups and sentences should be emphasized in teaching. The semantic structures include the following types: 1) modification(饭店: hotel; 红茶: black tea; 很好: very well); 2) action-recipient(吃饭: have a meal; 看书: read a book); 3) action-complement (看见:see; 说得好: speak well); 4) coordination (身体: body; 喜欢: like); 5) topic-comment(身体好: the body is well; 经济落后: economy is underdeveloped), etc. The semantic structure of a sentence is mainly the relation of the topic and the comment. The topic indicates what or who, the already-known information or what is talked about the comment. The comment is about what the topic does or how it is, the make-known information and the statement about the topic. "Who/what-what it does/how it is" is the fixed format of Chinese basic sentences. The teaching of semantic structure is not based on the explanation of the theory, but on examples that enable the learners to understand.

12. The textbook is accompanied by *an Exercise Book* and *Teacher's Guide*, which places emphasis on reading and writing. The main exercise items include the memorization of strokes *Hanzi* components, writing of *Hanzi*, and reading comprehension. Listening and speaking exercises are usually done in class.

The author

第十六课　马先生在家吗？
Lesson Sixteen　Is Mr.Ma at Home?

一、部件　Components of *Hanzi*

1. 手部旁 the shǒu left side
   扌(打)（扌音 shǒu hand）(扌＝手)
2. 纟部旁 the sī left side
   纟(给)（纟音 sī silk）
3. 走部框 the zǒu frame
   辶(还)（辶音 zǒu walk; go by walk）(辶＝走)
4. 文部心 the wén centre
   (这)（文＝文）

二、生字和生词　New *zi* and *zi*-groups

1. 还 (hái)　　　　　also; still
2. 呢 (ne)　　　　　*a modal particle*
   还……没有……(呢)　have not (done sth.) yet
3. 办 (bàn)　　　　do; handle; manage
   办公　　　　　　handle official business
4. 室 (shì)　　　　　room
   办公室　　　　　office
   教室 (jiàoshì)　　classroom
5. 可 (kě)　　　　　can; may
6. 以 (yǐ)　　　　　with; by means of; in order to
   可以　　　　　　may; can; be able to
7. 给 (gěi)　　　　　give; for; to
8. 打 (dǎ)　　　　　do; beat; strike; hit
9. 电 (diàn)　　　　electricity; electronic
10. 话 (huà)　　　　word; talk; speak about
    说话　　　　　　speak; talk

1

	电话	telephone
	打电话	make a telephone call
11.	接 (jiē)	receive; answer
	接电话	answer the phone
12.	手 (shǒu)	hand
	手机	mobile phone; hand phone
13.	吧 (ba)	*a modal particle*
14.	码 (mǎ)	*a sign or thing indicating number; yard* (yd.)
	号码	number
	电话号码	telephone number
15.	客 (kè)	guest
	客人 (kèren)	visitor; guest; guest (at a hotel, etc.)
16.	气 (qì)	air; gas; breath
	客气 (kèqi)	polite; modest
	不客气	not at all; don't mention it

三、补充生词 Supplementary *zi*-groups

1.	办学	run a school
2.	以来	since
3.	可是	but
4.	打工	do manual work
5.	电子 (diànzǐ)	electron
6.	请客	invite guest to dinner; treat
7.	司机	driver
8.	天气	weather
9.	气候	climate
10.	生气	get angry
11.	小气 (xiǎoqi)	stingy; mean

四、语音练习 Pronunciation Exercises

1. 声母练习 Initials practice

(1) 打 电 到 的 (d)

(2) 他 她 同 体 太 (t)

(3) 年 您 哪 你 女 那 呢 (n)

(4) 来 零 老 两 乐 累 六 了 (l)

(5) 高 工 公 国 给 广 个 贵 过 （g）
(6) 康 可 口 看 客 快 （k）
(7) 还 和 回 海 好 很 号 候 会 话 （h）

2. 音节识读 Read aloud the following syllables

dǎ（打）　diàn（电）　gěi（给）　hái（还）　kě（可）　kè（客）
ne（呢）　qì（气）　shǒu（手）　yǐ（以）

五、唱读和口译 Read aloud and interpret

1. 还……没……(呢)
   还没有来(呢)
   还没有回来(呢)
   还没有去(呢)
   还没有回去(呢)
   还没有看(呢)
   还没有看见(呢)

2. 打
   打电话
   打手机

3. 给
   给他打电话
   给他办公室打电话

4. 号码
   电话号码
   手机号码

六、会话 Dialogue

马先生在家吗？

三　木：您是马太太吗？马太太您好！我是三木。马先生在家吗？

马太太：您好，三木先生。马先生不在家，他还没有回来呢。

三　木：他在公司吗？

马太太：是，他在办公室，你可以给他办公室打电话。

三　木：他办公室的电话没人接。

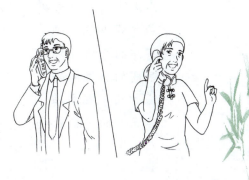

马太太：您打他的手机吧,他的手机号码是13301010788。
三　木：谢谢!
马太太：不客气!

七、替换练习 Substitution drills

1. 他还没有<u>回来</u>呢。
   回家
   去公司
   看见你
   去过天安门广场

2. 你可以给他<u>办公室</u>打电话。
   家
   公司
   父亲
   母亲

3. 您打<u>他的手机</u>吧。
   他公司的电话
   他办公室的电话
   他家的电话

4. 他<u>办公室</u>的电话没人接。
   家
   公司
   父亲
   母亲
   那儿

5. <u>他的手机号码</u>是13301010788。
   马太太的手机号码
   马先生的手机号码
   马建的手机号码
   马阳的手机号码
   王同的手机号码
   三木的手机号码
   林正美的手机号码

第十六课　马先生在家吗？

汉 语 知 识
Chinese Language ABC

1.汉字的造字方法（1）：象形字　Ways of formation of *Hanzi*（1）：the pictographic *zi*

在最早的汉字中,有些是用线条描画出来的代表人或事物形状的象形符号,用代表人或事物形状的象形符号表示意思。后来人们把这些代表人或事物形状的汉字叫做象形字。例如：

Among the earliest *Hanzi*, some were originally pictures of objects. Later people called them pictographic *zi*, whose meanings are indicated by objects' shapes. For example:

象形字发展到现在,字形已经发生了很大的变化,但是仍然保留着大致的轮廓,我们可以通过对字形的联想帮助记忆。

Up to now the pictographic *zi* have undergone great changes, but some are still recognizable so that we can memorize them by associating their forms.

2.字义例解和部件释义　Explanation of the meanings of *Hanzi* and *Hanzi* components

（1）纟。"纟"是"糸"作部旁时的简化形式,只作义符,作部底时写做"糸"。"糸"的古字 像一束丝。有"纟"（糸）作部件的汉字,其意思多半与织物以及丝、线、绳、纺织等有关。

"纟"(sī: silk) is the simplified form of the *zi* for "糸" when used as a left meaning component. And it's written as "糸" when used as a bottom component. The ancient form of the *zi* for "纟" resembles a floss of silk. The meanings of *Hanzi* with "纟"（糸）as a component are probably related to textile, silk, thread, rope, spinning and weaving, etc.

（2）气。"气"的古字 像云气上腾之形,代表气体。

The ancient form of the zi for "气" is similar to the shape of rising floating thin clouds.

(3) 手。"手"的古字 ⼿ 像张开的手掌,以手掌的形状代表"手"。

The ancient form of the *zi* for "手" resembles a spread palm, the shape of which stands for "手".

(4) 扌。"扌"是"手"作部旁时的变体,叫"扌(手)部旁",只作义符。凡带"扌(手)部旁"的汉字,其意思多半与手的动作或其他动作有关。

"扌" is the variant of "手" when used as a left meaning component. *Hanzi* with "扌" are mostly action-*zi* related to the action of hand or some other actions.

(5) 辶。"辶"的古字同"辵",像用脚在路上行走。在现代汉字中只作部框,叫"辶(走)部框",用做义符。凡带"辶(走)部框"的汉字,其意思多半与行走、距离等有关。

"辶" with the ancient form "辵" (chuò) means walking on the road. In modern *Hanzi*, it is only used as an enclosing meaning component called "走部框" (the zǒu frame). Meanings of *Hanzi* with "辶" as a component are often related to walking, distance, etc.

(6) 以。"以"的古字 ⼰ 像人在使用一种农具,意为"用"。

The ancient form of the *zi* for "以" resembles a person using a sort of farming tool, meaning "用" (yòng: use). It's an indicative *zi*.

(7) 话。"话"由"讠"(言)和"舌"组成。"讠"(言)即说话,说话必须用"舌",以"讠"(言)和"舌"的组合代表话语。

"话" (huà: word) is composed of "讠"(言) (yán: speak) and "舌" (shé: tongue). "讠"(言) is to speak, because people must speak with their tongues. The combination of "讠"(言) and "舌" stands for speech, remark.

3. 字词用法例解 Explanation of the usages of *zi* and *zi*-groups

(1) **他还没回来呢**。"呢"在这里表示肯定的语气。

"呢" here expresses an affirmative tone.

(2) **你打他的手机吧**。"吧"在这里表示提议和商量的语气。

"吧" here expresses the tone of advice or talking over.

(3) **他的手机号码是** 13301010788。数字"0"读"líng";在电话、手机、房间等的号码中,数字"1"读"yāo"。

The figure "0" is pronounced as "líng", while in phone, mobile phone and room numbers, "1" should be pronounced as "yāo".

第十七课　请你替我向她问好
Lesson Seventeen　Please Say Hello to Her

一、部件　Components of *Hanzi*

1. 火部旁 the huǒ left side
   火（烦）(火 huǒ fire)(火 = 火)
2. 车部旁 the chē left side
   车（辅）(车 chē vehicle)(车 = 车)
3. 食部旁 the shí left side
   饣(饭) (饣 shí food) (饣 = 食)

二、生字和生词　New *zi* and *zi*-groups

1. 替 (tì)　　　　　　replace; substitute
2. 向 (xiàng)　　　　direction; turn towards; to
3. 问 (wèn)　　　　　ask
   问好　　　　　　　say hello to
   向……问好　　　　say hello to sb.
4. 久 (jiǔ)　　　　　be long (time)
   长久　　　　　　　prolonged; lasting
   很久　　　　　　　be very long (time)
   不久　　　　　　　soon; before long; not long after
   好久　　　　　　　很久
   好久不见　　　　　have not met with each other for a long time
5. 忙 (máng)　　　　be busy
   很忙　　　　　　　be very busy
   工作很忙　　　　　be very busy with work
   不太忙　　　　　　be not so busy
   大忙人　　　　　　busy bee (a very busy person)
6. 白 (bái)　　　　　white
   白天　　　　　　　day (time between dawn to dusk)

7

7.	晚 (wǎn)	evening; night; night time; late (for sth.)
	晚上 (wǎnshang)	evening; (at) night
8.	要 (yào)	must; need; want; be going to; be about to
	还要	also need
9.	辅 (fǔ)	assist; supplement
10.	导 (dǎo)	lead; guide
	辅导	coach; give guidance in study or traning
11.	敢 (gǎn)	dare; be brave enough
	不敢	not dare to do sth.
12.	麻 (má)	rough
13.	烦 (fán)	be annoyed; be tired of
	麻烦 (máfan)	troublesome; inconvenient
14.	妈 (mā)	母亲
	妈妈	妈
15.	吃 (chī)	eat
	好吃 (hǎochī)	be delicious; be good to eat
	好吃 (hàochī)	enjoy eating
16.	饭 (fàn)	cooked rice or other cereals; meal
	吃饭	eat; have a meal

※ ※ ※ ※ ※

	太好了	wonderful; excellent

三、补充生词 Supplementary *zi*-groups

1.	问安	(*usu. to elders*) pay one's respects; wish sb. good health
2.	白日	(white) sun; day time
3.	晚安	good evening; good night
4.	晚了	be late (for sth.)
5.	不晚	be not late
6.	导师	tutor; teacher; guide of a great cause
7.	敢想敢说	dare to think and dare to act
8.	敢说敢做	dare to speak and dare to act
9.	请客吃饭	invite a guest to dinner
10.	吃不下	be unable to eat any more
11.	早饭	breakfast
12.	中饭	lunch

第十七课 请你替我向她问好

13. 晚饭　　　　　　　　supper; dinner
14. 晚年　　　　　　　　old age; one's later years

四、语音练习 Pronunciation Exercises

1. 韵母练习 Final practice

(1) 我 说 国 昨 过 作 做 坐 (wo, -uo)
(2) 回 会 贵 (wei, -ui)
(3) 安 三 先 烦 敢 办 饭 见 建 健 看 (an, -an)
(4) 康 长 常 忙 场 奖 上 (-ang)
(5) 今 亲 您 (-in)
(6) 英 京 经 星 名 明 请 病 姓 幸 兴 (ying, -ing)

2. 音节识读 Read aloud the following syllables

dǎo（导）　dào（到）　hǎo（好）　huí（回）　huì（会）　guì（贵）
gǎn（敢）　guó（国）　guò（过）　kàn（看）　wǎn（晚）
wáng（王）　wǒ（我）　jīn（今）　qīn（亲）　nín（您）
yào（要）　yīng（英）　jīng（京经）　xīng（星）
xìng（兴 姓 幸）　qǐng（请）　tì（替）　tiān（天）

五、唱读和口译 Read aloud and interpret

1. 向……问好
   向她问好
   向老师问好
   向大家问好
   向你父母问好

2. 好
   好久
   好几天
   好长时间
   好几个人

3. 好久
   好久不见了
   好久没来了
   好久没看见王同了
   好久没去过上海了

4. 要

    人人都要吃饭

    白天要工作,晚上还要学习

    明天要去上海

    星期天要去看王教授

5. 麻烦

    太麻烦

    麻烦您了

    不敢麻烦您

6. 请你……

    请你吃饭

    请你去上海

    请你辅导汉语

7. 不敢

    不敢麻烦你

    不敢见你

    不敢给你打电话

    不敢请你吃饭

六、会话 Dialogue

请你替我向她问好

马　建:林小姐,你好,我是马建。

林小姐:马先生,你好。

马　建:好久不见了,你工作忙吗?

林小姐:白天工作很忙,晚上还要学习。

马　建:你晚上学习什么?

林小姐:学习汉语,我的汉语不好。

马　建:要我辅导吗?

林小姐:你是个大忙人,我不敢麻烦你。

马　建:我妈妈要给你打电话,她想请你吃饭。

林小姐:是吗?太好了!谢谢她,请你替我向她问好。

七、替换练习 Substitution drills

1. 好久不见了,<u>你工作忙吗</u>?
   你身体好吗
   你去哪儿了
2. 我妈妈<u>要给你打电话</u>。
   要来看我
   要请你吃饭
   要坐飞机去上海
3. 她想<u>请你吃饭</u>。
   请你辅导汉语
   给你打电话
   来北京学习汉语
   去上海看朋友
   有个好工作
4. 请你替我向<u>她</u>问好。
   王教授
   马太太
   林小姐

Chinese Language ABC

1. 汉字的造字方法(2):指事字 Ways of formation of *Hanzi*(2): the indicative *zi*

在最早的汉字中,有些是用线条描画出来的代表人或事物特点的象形符号,用代表人或事物特点的象形符号表示意思。后来人们把这类代表人或事物特点的象形符号叫做指事字。例如:

Originally some *Hanzi* were pictures to highlight the characteristics of sth. Later they were known as indicative *zi*. For example:

一、二、三:用不同数量的横线表示不同的数目。

一、二、三: The different number of horizontal lines show different numbers.

中:在"口"的中央加"丨"表示位置居中。

中："丨"(the vertical line) descending through the middle of "口" shows being in the middle, centre.

王：古字像大斧，象征帝王的权力，以此代表帝王。

The ancient form of the *zi* for "王" resembles a big axe, standing for the king's power. So it represents a king.

本：在"木"的下部加一个符号表示树根。引申义为根本。

本：The line added at the bottom of "木" shows that it's the root of a tree. Its extended meaning is fundamentality. It's an indicative *zi*.

2. 字义例解和部件释义 Explanation of the meanings of *Hanzi* and *Hanzi* components

（1）车。象形字。"车"是"車"的简化字，作部旁时写作"车"。"車"的古字"車"中间的"曰"像车厢。有"车"(车)作部件的汉字，其意思多与车辆、运输等有关。

"车"（chē: vehicle）is the simplified form of "車". When used as a left component, it's written as "车". "曰" in the middle of "車" is like a carriage. Meanings of *Hanzi* with "车"（车）as a left component are often related to vehicles or transportation, etc. "車" is a pictographic *zi*.

（2）火。"火"的古字像火焰的形状，作部旁时写作"灬"。象形字。

The ancient *Hanzi* "火"（huǒ: fire）is like the shape of flame. When used as a left component, it's written as "灬". It's a pictographic *zi*.

（3）白。"白"的古字像太阳即将升起，这时东方呈白色。指事字。

The ancient form of the *zi* for "白" resembles the rising sun when the sky turns white. It's an indicative *zi*.

（4）饣。"饣"是"食"作部旁时的简化形式，用做义符。有"饣"(食)作部件的汉字，其意思多半与饮食有关。"食"的古字碗里盛满食物，上有盖。用碗上有盖代表食物，是因为食物可以盛在碗里，可以在碗上加盖保温、保洁。指事字。

"饣"（shí: food）is the simplified form of the *zi* for "食" when used as a left meaning component. *Hanzi* with "饣"（食）as a component are often related to food and drink. The ancient form of the *zi* for "食" resembles a bowl full of food, with a cover on the top, for food in bowl with a cover can keep warm and clean. It's an indicative *zi*.

（5）饭。"饭"由"饣"和"反"组成，"饣"是义符。"反"是音符（"饭"和"反"声调不同）。

"饭" is composed of "饣" and "反"（fǎn: counter），with "饣" as the meaning component and "反" as the sound（"饭" and "反" are in different tones）.

第十七课　请你替我向她问好

(6) 问。"问"由"门"和"口"组成。"口"是义符,代表发问;"门"是音符("问"和"门"韵母相同)。

"问" is composed of "门" and "口", with "口" as the meaning component, standing for questioning and "门" as the sound indicating the pronunciation ("问" and "门" share the same final).

3. 字词用法例解　Explanation of the usages of *zi* and *zi*-groups

(1) 好久不见了。也可以说"好久不见"或"好久没见了"。这里的"好"是"很、很多"的意思,"好久"就是"很长时间"。还可以说"好几天"(意为"很多天"),"好几个月"(意为很多个月),"好几个人"(意为很多人)。"几"代表"十"以内的数目,前面加"好"就是强调时间长或数量大。

Also say "好久不见" or "好久没见了". Here "好" means "very, many(much)", then "好久" is "very long time". More examples are "好几天" (many days), "好几个月" (many months), "好几个人" (a good number of people). "几" represents the number within ten and "好" preceding "几" is to emphasize a long time or a large number.

(2) 是吗? 这是用于确认事实的问话,有时只是表示"知道了",并非问话。所以可以回答"是",也可以不答。

It is a question to confirm the fact. Sometimes it only expresses "knowing" instead of a real question, so the speaker does not expect an answer, but the listener can answer with "是" (yes).

(3) 太好了! 用于赞扬某事或某人非常好,并表示一种兴奋的心情。后面常常用叹号(!)。

It is used to praise something or someone in excitement. It's often followed by an exclamation mark (!).

第十八课　我想请你吃午饭
Lesson Eighteen
I would Like to Invite You to Lunch

一、部件　Components of *Hanzi*

1. 矢部旁 the shǐ side
   矢（知）(矢 shǐ arrow)(矢=矢)
2. 火部底 the huǒ bottom
   灬（点）(火 huǒ fire)(灬=火)
3. 手部心 the shǒu centre
   ⺘（用）(⺘=手)
4. 用部框 the yòng frame
   冂（用）(冂音 yòng)

二、生字和生词　New *zi* and *zi*-groups

1. 午 (wǔ)　　　　　noon; midday
   上午　　　　　　morning
   中午　　　　　　noon
   下午　　　　　　afternoon
   午饭　　　　　　中饭
   吃午饭　　　　　have lunch
2. 最 (zuì)　　　　　most; best
   最大　　　　　　largest; greatest
   最小　　　　　　least; smallest
   最高　　　　　　highest; tallest
   最好　　　　　　best; first-rate; had better; it would be better
3. 近 (jìn)　　　　　be near; be close to
   很近　　　　　　be very close
   最近　　　　　　recently; the near future; nearest
4. 比 (bǐ)　　　　　compare; contrast; than

第十八课　我想请你吃午饭

5. 较 (jiào)　　　　　compare; contrast
   比较　　　　　　compare; fairly; comparatively
6. 间 (jiān)　　　　　within a definite time or space; between; *a measure-zi*
   中间　　　　　　among; between; centre; middle
   时间　　　　　　time
7. 应 (yīng)　　　　　should; ought to
8. 该 (gāi)　　　　　ought to be; should be
   应该　　　　　　should; ought to
9. 点 (diǎn)　　　　　o'clock; point; drop; dot; put a dot
   几点　　　　　　what time (is it)
   十二点　　　　　twelve o'clock
10. 怎 (zěn)　　　　　why; how
    怎么　　　　　　why; how
11. 样 (yàng)　　　　 appearance; shape; sample; model
    怎么样　　　　　how; what; how are things; what do you think
    身体怎么样　　　how is (one's) health
12. 店 (diàn)　　　　　shop; store
    饭店　　　　　　hotel; restaurant
    北京饭店　　　　Beijing Hotel
13. 知 (zhī)　　　　　know; be aware (of)
    知识 (zhīshi)　　knowledge; intellect
14. 道 (dào)　　　　　way; road; path; say; talk; speak
    知道　　　　　　know; realize; be aware of
15. 关 (guān)　　　　 shut; close; concern; involve
    关门　　　　　　close (the door)
16. 系 (xì)　　　　　 relate to; bear on
    关系　　　　　　connections; relationship
    没关系　　　　　it doesn't matter
    　　※　※　※　※　※
    好像　　　　　　seem; be like
    不过　　　　　　but
    问人　　　　　　ask

三、补充生词　Supplementary *zi*-groups

1. 午安　　　　　　good noon
2. 样子 (yàngzi)　　appearance; shape; sample

3. 一样   the same; alike
4. 怎样   怎么样
5. 这样   like this
6. 那样   of that kind; like that; such; so
7. 书店   bookstore
8. 关心   be concerned with; care for
9. 海关   customs

四、语音练习 Pronunciation Exercises

1. 声母练习 Initials practice

(1) 八 白 北 比 办 病 不 吧 (b)
(2) 麻 忙 没 门 明 马 免 母 木 吗 么 (m)
(3) 飞 非 烦 辅 父 饭 (f)
(4) 中 专 这 祝 (zh)
(5) 吃 长 常 场 (ch)
(6) 师 生 书 说 十 时 识 谁 什 手 寿 室 上 (sh)
(7) 人 认 日 (r)

2. 音节识读 Read aloud the following syllables

běi（北）　bǐ（比）　diǎn（点）　fàn（饭）　gāi（该）　guān（关）
jìn（近）　mā（妈）　má（麻）　mǎ（马码）　ma（吗）　me（么）
yàng（样）　zhī（知）　zěn（怎）　zuì（最）　chī（吃）　shí（十时）
shì（是）　wǔ（五午）　rì（日）　xì（系）　Běijīng（北京）
fàndiàn（饭店）　zuìjìn（最近）　zěnmeyàng（怎么样）

五、唱读和口译 Read aloud and interpret

1. 饭
   早饭
   吃早饭
   午饭(中饭)
   吃午饭(吃中饭)
   晚饭
   吃晚饭
2. 应该
   应该做
   这是我应该做的

应该去北语学汉语

应该我请你

3. 点

几点

上午八点

中午十二点

晚上六点

4. 好像

好像在长安街

好像要生病

好像有你的电话

好像是马阳

5. 见

再见

晚上见

下午见

明天见

星期六见

六、会话 Dialogue

我想请你吃午饭

王明英：是林小姐吗？我是王明英。

林正美：马太太，您好！

王明英：林小姐，好久不见了，你最近忙吗？

林正美：比较忙，马太太最近身体好吗？

王明英：我身体很好。林小姐，我和我先生想请你和三木先生吃午饭，你有时间吗？

林正美：您太客气了！应该我请您。什么时候？

王明英：星期六中午十二点，怎么样？

林正美：太好了！在哪儿呢？

王明英：在北京饭店，你知道北京饭店在哪儿吗？

林正美：我没去过，好像在长安街。不过没关系，我可以问人。谢谢您。

王明英：不用客气，星期六见。

林正美：星期六见。

七、替换练习 Substitution drills

1. 我想请你吃饭,你有时间吗?
   我想去看你
   我想请你辅导汉语
2. 星期六中午十二点,怎么样?
   晚上六点吃晚饭
   去北京饭店吃饭
   你一个人去
3. 你知道北京饭店在哪儿吗?
   长安街
   天安门广场
   马先生家
   北京大学
4. 不过没关系,我可以问人。
   我可以请马阳辅导
   我可以一个人去
   我可以坐飞机去

1. 汉字的造字方法(3):会意字 Ways of formation of *Hanzi* (3): the ideographic *zi*

用象形符号的组合提示字义的汉字叫做会意字。例如:

Those *Hanzi* that express meanings by combination of picture signs are ideographic *zi*. For example:

(1) 明。由"日"和"月"组成,"日"和"月"是代表事物形状的象形字,因为它们都能显示光亮,所以用来代表光亮、光明。

"明" is composed of "日" (rì: sun) and "月" (yuè: moon), which both stand for their shapes. Therefore they can express the brightness, standing for light and brightness.

第十八课　我想请你吃午饭

(2) 国。由"囗"和"玉"组成,"囗"是包围的样子,"玉"的古字像一串玉,它们都是代表事物形状的象形字,分别代表边界和财宝,用有边界和财宝的地方代表国家。

"国" is composed of "囗" (wéi: enclose) and "玉" (yù: jade). "囗" is like an enclosure, and the ancient form of the *zi* for "玉" stands for a string of jade. They are pictographic *zi* and stand for borderline and treasure respectively. A place with treasure and fixed borderline represents a country.

(3) 家。由"宀"和"豕"组成,"宀"像房顶的形状,代表房屋,"豕"像猪的形状,代表猪,用房子里有猪代表家。

"家" is composed of "宀" and "豕". "宀" looks like the shape of the roof of a house, standing for house. "豕" has the shape of a pig, representing the pig. To raise pigs in the house stands for home.

(4) 安。"安"由"宀"和"女"组成。"宀"代表屋子,"女"即女人,用女人在屋子里代表安全。

"安" (ān: peaceful) is formed of "宀" and "女". "宀" represents a house, and "女" means woman. "A woman under the roof" means safety, stability.

(5) 时。由"日"和"寸"组成。"寸"在这里有测量的意思,用测量太阳的位置表示记时。

"时" is made of "日" and "寸" (cùn: *a unit of length*). Here "寸" means measuring. To measure the sun's position is to measure the time.

2. **字义例解和部件释义 Explanation of the meanings of *Hanzi* and *Hanzi* components**

(1) 比。"比"(𠤎𠤎)由两个"匕"组成。二匕并列,表示相比。会意字。

"比" is formed of two "匕" (bǐ: spoon). To put two "匕" together indicates comparison. It's an ideographic *Hanzi*.

(2) 灬。"灬"是4"火"用作部底时的变体,叫火部底,只作义符。"火"的古字像火焰的形状,代表"火"。有"灬"(火)作部件的汉字,其意思多与"火、燃烧、炎热"等有关。

"灬", named the huǒ bottom, is the variant of "火" (huǒ: fire) when used as a bottom meaning component. The ancient form of the *zi* for "火" resembles the shape of a blazing fire. *Hanzi* with "灬" (火) are often related to fire, burn, burning hot, etc. in meaning.

(3) 点。"点"由"占"和"灬"组成,"灬"(火)是义符,"占"是音符("点"和"占"韵母相近),意为"点燃"。也是"时点、地点"等的"点"。

"点" is composed of "占" (zhàn: occupy) and "灬"（火）(huǒ: fire). "灬"（火）is the meaning component, and "占" the sound component ("点" and "占" have similar finals). "点" means "点燃" (diǎnrán: light; ignite). It also means o'clock (时点) and place (地点), etc.

(4) 店。"店"由"广"和"占"组成,"广"代表房屋,是义符,"占"是音符("店"和"占"声调相同,韵母相近,声母不同)。

"店" is composed of "广" and "占" (zhàn: occupy). "广" stands for a house and is a meaning element, while "占" a sound element ("店" and "占" share the same tone, with the similar final but with different initials).

(5) 矢。"矢"是"矢"作部旁时的普体。"矢"的古字像头朝上的箭,以"箭"的形状代表"箭"。

"矢" (shǐ: arrow) is the variant of "矢" when used as a component. The top of the ancient form of the zi for "矢" is like an arrow with the head up. The shape of the arrow stands for arrow.

(6) 知。"知"由"矢"和"口"组成。"矢"的速度很快,代表敏捷,"口"代表"问"。敏捷、好问就能知晓。

"知" is composed of "矢" and "口". "矢"（矢）is fast speed and stands for smartness and "口" represents questioning. Being smart and questioning could help one get more knowledge.

(7) 道。"道"由"首"和"辶"组成。"首"的古字像人头,以人头的形状代表头。"辶"即行走,行走时的地方是道路。引申义有"规律、解说"等。会意字。

"道" is composed of "首" (shǒu: head) and "辶" (zǒu: go; walk). The ancient form of the zi for "首" is like a person's head. The shape of the head stands for head. "辶" is to walk. Later it was extended to mean "规律" (guīlǜ: law; regular pattern), "解说" (jiěshuō: explain orally; comment), etc. It's an ideographic zi.

3. 字词用法例解 Explanation of the usages of zi and zi-groups

好像…… 用于表示虽然知道,但是没有把握。
"好像……" is used to express uncertainty despite of awareness.

第十九课　北京饭店在哪儿?
Lesson Nineteen　Where is Beijing Hotel?

一、部件 Components of *Hanzi*

1. 金部旁 the jīn left side
   钅(钟)（钅＝金）(金 jīn gold)
2. 立部旁 the lì left side
   立(站)（立＝立）(立 lì stand)
3. 阝部边 the yì right side
   阝(那)（阝＝邑）(邑 yì city)
4. 走部底 the zǒu bottom
   (走)（走音 zǒu)(走 zǒu walk)（辶＝走）

二、生字和生词 New *zi* and *zi*-groups

1. 南 (nán)　　　　south
   南京　　　　　　Nanjing (the *capital of Jiangsu Province*)
2. 面 (miàn)　　　face; surface; side
   南面　　　　　　south; the south
   见面　　　　　　meet
3. 走 (zǒu)　　　　walk; (go by walk); leave
   怎么走　　　　　how to go
4. 东 (dōng)　　　east
   东面　　　　　　the east
   东京　　　　　　Tokyo (capital of Japan)
5. 从 (cóng)　　　follow; join; from
   从……向……　　go… from…
   从……到……　　from… to…
6. 西 (xī)　　　　west
   西面　　　　　　the west
   西安　　　　　　Xi'an (*the capital of Shanxi province*)

21

7.	离 (lí)	leave; be away from; part from
8.	共 (gòng)	common; general; altogether; in all
	公共	public; common
9.	汽 (qì)	vapour; steam
10.	车 (chē)	vehicle
	汽车	automobile; motor vehicle; car
	公共汽车	public bus
11.	站 (zhàn)	stand; stop; station
	车站	stop; station
12.	多 (duō)	many; much; more
	很多	many; much
	多长	how long
	多长时间	how long time
	多大	how old (asking the age)
	多谢	many thanks
13.	能 (néng)	can; be able to
	能到	can arrive
14.	分 (fēn)	minute; divide
	分公司	branch of a company
15.	钟 (zhōng)	bell; clock
	分钟	minute
	二十分钟	twenty minutes
	点钟	o'clock
	两点钟	two o'clock
16.	那 (nà)	that
	那儿	there
17.	的 (dī)	*short form for* "的士"(díshī: taxi)
	打的 (dǎ dī)	take a taxi

※ ※ ※ ※ ※

	请问	may I ask
	要是	if

三、补充生词 Supplementary *zi*-groups

1.	面向	turn one's face to; face
2.	面子	outer part; face
3.	向西	towards west

第十九课　北京饭店在哪儿？

4. 西北　　　　　　　　northwest
5. 东南　　　　　　　　southeast
6. 东西 (dōngxi)　　　　thing; stuff
7. 南门　　　　　　　　south gate
8. 共同　　　　　　　　common; shared; jointly
9. 一共　　　　　　　　altogether; in all
10. 可能　　　　　　　　possible; maybe
11. 分离　　　　　　　　leave each other; separate; part

四、语音练习　Pronunciation Exercises

1. 声母练习 Initials practice
（1）本 朋（b p）
（2）早 从（z c）

2. 韵母练习 Finals practice
（1）分 门 人 很 认（-en）
（2）生 能 朋（-eng）
（3）东 工 公 中 钟 从 同 共（-ong）
（4）晚 关 专（wan, -uan）
（5）王 广（wang, -uang）

3. 音节识读 Read aloud the following Syllables

péng（朋）　mián（面）　fēn（分）
dōng（东）　dī（的）　de（的）　duō（多）
nà（那）　nán（南）　néng（能）
lí（离）　gòng（共）　qì（气汽）　xī（西）
zhàn（站）　zhōng（中钟）　chē（车）　cóng（从）
zài（在再）　zǒu（走）

五、唱读和口译　Read aloud and interpret

1. 面
   东面
   西面
   南面
   北面
   上面
   下面

2. 从……向……
   从这儿向西
   从天安门广场向南
   从北京大学南门向东
   从南京向北

3. 从……到……
   从南京到北京
   从上海到西安
   从韩国到日本
   从中国到美国

4. 什么时候？
   上午八点
   下午四点
   晚上九点
   两点十分
   六点二十分

5. 多长时间？
   二十分钟
   一个小时
   二十四个小时
   两个小时四十分钟

六、会话 Dialogue

北京饭店在哪儿？

A：小姐，请问，北京饭店在哪儿？
B：北京饭店吗？我也不知道，好像在南面。
A：谢谢！
B：不客气！
A：先生，麻烦您，去北京饭店怎么走？
B：北京饭店在天安门广场东面，您可以从这儿向西。
A：离这儿远不远？
B：不太远，您可以坐公共汽车，车站就在那儿。
A：要是坐公共汽车，多长时间能到？
B：从这儿到北京饭店，二十分钟吧。打的比较快，十分钟就到。
A：多谢！
B：不谢！

第十九课　北京饭店在哪儿?

七、替换练习　Substitution drills

1. 请问,<u>北京饭店</u>在哪儿?
   天安门广场
   王教授家
   马先生的公司
   林正美小姐

2. <u>北京饭店</u>离这儿远不远?
   长安街
   天安门广场
   马太太家
   你们的公司

3. 北京饭店离这儿<u>不太远</u>。
   很远
   不远

4. 你可以<u>坐公共汽车</u>。
   去问王教授
   给他打电话
   请马阳辅导

5. <u>坐公共汽车</u>多长时间能到?
   打的
   去天安门广场
   去马太太家
   去你们的公司

6. <u>打的比较快,十分钟就到</u>。
   坐飞机比较快,两个小时就到
   坐公共汽车比较快,二十分钟就到

1. 汉字的造字方法（4）：形声字 Ways of formation of *Hanzi* （4）：the pictophonetic *zi*

由义符和音符组成的汉字叫形声字。形声字的义符代表义类，音符代表音类。我们已学过一些带全表音和半表音音符的形声字。例如：

Picto-phonetic *zi*. *Hanzi* that are composed of a meaning component and a phonetic component are the picto-phonetic *zi*. The meaning component stands for the meaning type of the *Hanzi* and the phonetic component For the sound type. For example:

1.1 带全表音音符的形声字 Picto-phonetic *zi* with the full phonetic component

比　比
禾　和
里　理
马　码
气　汽
受　授
象　像
占　站
中　钟

1.2 带半表音音符的形声字 Picto-phonetic *zi* with the half phonetic element

几　机
马　妈　吗
那　哪
十　什
门　们

2. 字义例解和部件释义 Explanation of the meanings of *Hanzi* and *Hanzi* components

（1）面。"面"的古字像人的脸面。象形字。

The ancient form of the *zi* for "面" resembles a person's face. It's a pictographic *zi*.

（2）东。"东"是"東"的简化字。"東"的古字像日在木中，木代表树林，表示从树林看到的刚刚升起的太阳是在东方。指事字。

"东"（dōng: east）is the simplified *Hanzi* of "東"，the ancient form of the *Hanzi* for 东（東）is like the sun in the mid of trees representing wood. It means that the rising sun over the wood is in the east. It's an ideographic *zi*.

（3）多。"多"由两个"夕"组成，"夕"的古字同"月"。"多"即两个月亮，意为多出了一个。

"多"（duō: more）is composed of two "夕"。The ancient form of the *Hanzi* for "夕" is the same as that of "月"。So "多" are two moons, meaning there is an extra moon.

（4）从。"从"由两个"人"组成，两个人一前一后，代表跟从。会意字。

"从" is formed of two "人"，one following the other, meaning "to follow". It's an ideographic *zi*.

（5）分。"分"由"八"和"刀"组成。"八"由相反的两个笔画组成，最初是"分"的意思。"刀"表示"用刀切开"，在这里代表"分"的手段。会意字。引申义为"区分"（distinguish），借用为时间单位"分"（minute）和货币单位"分"（equal to one hundredth of a yuan）等。

"分" is composed of "八" and "刀"（dāo: knife）。"八" formed by two opposite strokes originally means separation. "刀" denotes "divide" with a knife. "分" is an ideographic *Hanzi* and its extended meaning is "区分 (distinguish)"， and it is also borrowed to mean "分"，both a unit of time (minute) and of currency (equal to 1% of a yuan).

（6）立。"立"的古字像人在地上正面站立的样子，以此代表站立。指事字。

The ancient form of the *zi* for "立"（lì: stand）is like a person standing on the ground. This therefore represents standing. It's a self-explanatory *zi*.

（7）站。"站"的本义是"站立"，由"立"（立）和"占"组成，"立"是义符，"占"是全表音音符。形声字。

The original meaning of ("站" is "to stand")，composed of "立"（立）and "占"（zhàn）。"立" is the meaning component and "占" the full sound component. It's an picto-phonetic *zi*.

(8) 钟。"钟"由"钅"和"中"组成。"钅"是"金"作部旁时的简化形式,代表金属,用做义符,表示"钟"由金属制成。"中"是全表音音符。形声字。

"钟" is composed of "钅" and "中". "钅" is the simplified form of "金" (jīn: gold) when used as a left component, standing for metal. "钅" is the meaning component and indicates that "钟" is made of metal. "中" is the full sound component. It's a picto- phonetic *zi*.

(9) 阝。阝=邑,用做部边。以"阝"做部边的汉字,其意思多与地方、地域、姓氏(古人常以所在地的地名为姓)等有关。

"阝" (yì: city) is equal to "邑 (yì: city)". It's often used on the right of a *Hanzi*. Meanings of *Hanzi* with "阝" as a right meaning components are related to a place, large areas, surnames (in ancient times people often took the place they lived in as their surnames), etc.

3. 字词用法例解 Explanation of the usages of *zi* and *zi*-groups

(1) 请问。"请问"是"我问你"的意思,这是向别人打听某人或某事时的客气问法。例如:

"请问" means "I ask you". It's a polite question to ask others about someone or something. For example:

① 请问,三木先生在这儿吗?
② 请问,北京饭店在哪儿?
③ 请问,去天安门广场怎么走?
④ 请问,这个汉字怎样写?(写:xiě: write)

(2) 就到。"就"可以用于表示动作行为发生的时间早、需要的时间短等。例如:

"就" can be used to express that actions occurred earlier and the short time needed. For example:

① 打的比较快,十分钟就到。
② 从北京去上海,坐飞机两个小时就到。
③ 我们是八点来的,他七点就来了。
④ 他们早就认识了。
⑤ 马太太还没到呢,马先生早就来了。

第二十课　复习(四)
Lesson Twenty　Review (4)

一、语音复习

1. 唱读下列汉字，注意声母的发音 Read aloud the following *Hanzi* and highlight the pronunciation of initials

   (1) 八 吧 白 办 北 比 本 病 不 (b)

   (2) 朋 (p)

   (3) 妈 麻 马 码 吗 忙 么 没 门 免 面 明 母 木 (m)

   (4) 烦 饭 飞 非 分 辅 父 (f)

   (5) 打 的 点 电 店 导 到 道 东 多 (d)

   (6) 他 她 太 体 替 同 (t)

   (7) 那 南 呢 年 您 哪 你 能 女 (n)

   (8) 来 两 老 乐 了 累 离 零 六 (l)

   (9) 该 敢 高 个 给 工 公 共 关 广 贵 国 过 (g)

   (10) 看 康 可 客 口 快 (k)

   (11) 还 海 好 号 和 很 候 话 回 会 (h)

   (12) 接 间 较 久 近 (j, ji)

   (13) 气 汽 (q, qi)

   (14) 西 系 向 (x, xi)

   (15) 知 这 站 祝 专 中 钟 (zh, zhi)

   (16) 吃 长 常 场 车 (ch, chi)

   (17) 师 十 时 识 室 上 谁 什 生 手 寿 书 说 (sh, shi)

   (18) 人 认 日 (r, ri)

   (19) 子 字 在 再 早 走 昨 作 做 最 总 (z, zi)

   (20) 从 (c, ci)

   (21) 厶 司 三 四 (s, si)

2. 唱读下列汉字，注意韵母的发音 Read aloud the following *Hanzi* and highlight the pronunciation of finals

   (1) 八 家 他 妈 马 码 吗 哪 那 (-a)

   (2) 的 和 个 乐 了 么 这 (-e)

(3) 一以样应几理你体七期习系 (yi, -i)

(4) 司四子 (-i)

(5) 十时识实是日 (-i)

(6) 五午不辅父母木书祝 (wu, -u)

(7) 语女去 (yu, -ü)

(8) 还海来太在再 (-ai)

(9) 北非飞累没谁 (-ei)

(10) 到老高好号早 (-ao)

(11) 候口寿 (-ou)

(12) 也业街姐谢 (ye, -ie)

(13) 话 (-ua)

(14) 我多国过说昨作做坐 (wo, -uo)

(15) 月学 (yue, -üe)

(16) 要叫教较小 (yao, -iao)

(17) 有友九久就六 (you, -iu)

(18) 快 (-uai)

(19) 贵回会最 (-ui, uei)

(20) 安办烦饭敢汉看三 (an, -an)

(21) 本分很门问人认 (-en)

(22) 言见建健免年天先 (yan, -ian)

(23) 今近您亲 (-in)

(24) 晚关专 (wan, -uan)

(25) 文问 (wen)

(26) 远 (yuan, -üan)

(27) 长常场康忙上 (-ang)

(28) 能朋生 (-eng)

(29) 从东工公共同中钟 (-ong)

(30) 阳奖两想像 (yang, -iang)

(31) 英病京经名明请星姓幸兴 (ying, -ing)

(32) 用 (yong)

(33) 王广 (wang, -uang)

(34) 儿二 (er)

二、部件复习：说出下列部件的名称 Tell the names of following components

1. 一(六)

第二十课 复习(四)

2. 宀(安)
3. 丷(美)
4. 八(分)
5. 耂(老)
6. 𠂇(有)
7. 手(看)
8. 朩(亲)
9. 匕(老)
10. 厶(去)
11. 灬(点)
12. 辶(走)
13. 口(名)
14. 日(替)
15. 小(系)
16. 亻(你)
17. 讠(谢)
18. 女(姓)
19. 氵(汉)
20. 扌(打)
21. 忄(快)
22. 木(机)
23. 火(烦)
24. 车(辅)
25. 饣(饭)
26. 矢(知)
27. 口(吃)
28. 日(晚)
29. 纟(给)
30. 钅(钟)
31. 立(站)
32. 刂(到)
33. 匕(比)
34. 生(姓)
35. 口(知)
36. 子(好)
37. 马(妈)

31

38. 气(汽)
39. 中(钟)
40. 丨(用)
41. 不(还)
42. 口(问)
43. 日(间)
44. 林(麻)
45. 辶(这)
46. 冂(用)
47. 门(问)
48. 广(店)

三、朗读下列常用语句 Read aloud the following frequently used sentences

您好！
幸会！
好久不见了！
您太客气了！
※ ※ ※ ※ ※
谢谢！
谢谢您！
多谢！
麻烦您了！
※ ※ ※ ※ ※
不谢！
不用谢！
不客气！
不用客气！
※ ※ ※ ※ ※
我想请你吃饭,你有时间吗？
请你替我向她问好。
小姐,请问,北京饭店在哪儿
先生,麻烦您,去北京饭店怎么走？

四、唱读下列电话号码和手机号码 Read aloud the following telephone numbers

82330891　　　　62301859　　　　86-10-62100518
13010107788　　　13189785418

五、说话练习 Oral practice

1. 说说(shuōshuo:说一下)三木给马太太打电话的情况(qíngkuàng: situation)。
   (1) 三木为什么给马太太打电话？
   (2) 马太太为什么告诉(gàosu: tell)三木马先生的手机号码？

2. 说说马建给林正美打电话的情况。
   (1) 马建认识林正美吗？你怎么知道？
   (2) 马建为什么给林正美打电话？
   (3) 他们在电话里说什么了？

3. 说说王明英给林正美打电话的情况。
   (1) 马太太叫什么名字？你怎么知道？
   (2) 林正美认识马太太吗？
   (3) 马太太为什么给林正美打电话？
   (4) 她们在电话里说什么了？

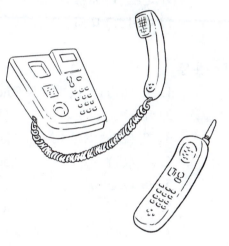

4. 说说去北京饭店的情况。
   (1) 谁去北京饭店了？你怎么知道？
   (2) 她知道去北京饭店怎么走吗？你怎么知道？
   (3) 她问了几个人？
   (4) 她问了些(xiē: some)什么问题(wèntí: question)？
   (5) 她有什么方法(fāngfǎ: way)去北京饭店？要多长时间？

六、说快板儿 Read and recite a clapper talk

部件歌
A rhyme of *Hanzi* components

上是头，八部头。
八刀分，丷天关。

下是底,心部底。
相心想,你心您。

左是旁,女部旁。
女马妈,女子好。

右是边,月部边。
日月明,月月朋。

内是心,口部心。
口口回,丁口可。

外是框,门部框。
门口问,门日间。

生字

1. 头 (tóu)   head; top
2. 部 (bù)   (*Hanzi*) radical
3. 刀 (dāo)   knife
4. 底 (dǐ)   bottom
5. 相 (xiāng)   each other; mutually
6. 左 (zuǒ)   left
7. 旁 (páng)   side (here: left side)
8. 右 (yòu)   right
9. 边 (biān)   side (here: right side)
10. 内 (nèi)   inside; inner
11. 外 (wài)   outside; outer
12. 框 (kuàng)   frame
13. 囗 (wéi)   enclose
14. 丁 (Dīng)   *a family name*

第二十一课
你们喝什么饮料？
Lesson Twenty-one
What Kind of Drinks Would You Like?

一、部件 Components of *Hanzi*

1. 草部头 the cǎo top
   艹(茶)(草 cǎo grass)(艹=草)
2. 采部底 the cǎi bottom
   采(菜)(采 cǎi pick)
3. 米部旁 the mǐ left side
   米(料)(米 mǐ shelled rice or other grains)(米=米)
4. 欠部边 the qiàn right side
   欠(欢)(欠 qiàn be short of)
5. 酉部边 the yǒu right side
   酉(酒)(酉 yǒu alcoholic beverage)

二、生字和生词 New *zi* and *zi*-groups

1. 喝 (hē)   drink
2. 饮 (yǐn)   喝
3. 料 (liào)   material; stuff
   饮料   beverage; drink
4. 菜 (cài)   vegetable; dish
5. 点 (diǎn)   select; choose; order
   点菜   order dishes (in a restaurant)
6. 服 (fú)   serve
7. 务 (wù)   be engaged in
   服务   serve; give service to
8. 员 (yuán)   *a person engaged in some field of activity*

服务员	attendant; waiter
9. 茶 (chá)	tea
喝茶	drink tea
10. 咖啡 (kāfēi)	coffee
喝咖啡	drink coffee
11. 杯 (bēi)	cup; *a measure-zi*
杯子	cup
12. 红 (hóng)	red
红茶	black tea
13. 绿 (lǜ)	green
绿茶	green tea
14. 喜 (xǐ)	like; happy; delighted; a happy event (esp. wedding)
15. 欢 (huān)	joyous; merry
喜欢 (xǐhuan)	like; love; be fond of
16. 龙 (lóng)	dragon
17. 井 (jǐng)	well
龙井(茶)	Longjing tea
18. 酒 (jiǔ)	alcoholic beverage; wine
红酒	wine
白酒	white spirit
19. 啤酒 (píjiǔ)	beer
20. 瓶 (píng)	bottle; vase; jar; *a measure-zi*
瓶子 (píngzi)	bottle

※ ※ ※ ※ ※

还是	or (used in questions)

三、补充生词 Supplementary *zi*-groups

1.	白菜	Chinese cabbage
2.	饭菜	meal
3.	公务	public affairs; official business
4.	公务员	public servant; civil servant; civil service
5.	饮茶	喝茶
6.	酒菜	wine and dishes; dishes to go with wine
7.	酒饭	wine and food
8.	酒店	wineshop; hotel

第二十一课　你们喝什么饮料？

9. 喜酒　　　　　wine offered at a wedding; wedding feast
10. (一)点儿　　　a bit; a little

四、唱读和口译　Read aloud and interpret

1. 喝
   喝茶
   喝红茶
   喝绿茶
   喝龙井
   喝咖啡
   喝酒
   喝红酒
   喝白酒
   喝啤酒

2. 喜欢
   喜欢林小姐
   喜欢中国
   喜欢看书
   喜欢喝茶
   喜欢喝酒
   喜欢在饭店吃饭

3. 瓶
   一瓶酒
   两瓶红酒
   三瓶啤酒

五、会话　Dialogue

你们喝什么饮料？

马太太：林小姐到了，我们点菜。
马　建：服务员，点菜。
马太太：你们喝什么饮料？
马先生：林小姐，你喝茶还是喝咖啡？
林小姐：我喝茶。
服务员：有红茶，也有绿茶，您喝红茶还是喝绿茶？
马　建：林小姐喜欢喝龙井。

马太太：太好了！我也喜欢龙井。三木先生呢？
三　木：我喝咖啡吧。
马先生：我也喝咖啡，要两杯咖啡。
马太太：你们不喝酒吗？
三　木：中午不能喝酒，下午还要工作。
马先生：要两瓶啤酒吧。
马　建：再要一瓶红酒吧，我妈和林小姐都能喝红酒。

六、替换练习 Substitution drills

1. 你们喝什么<u>饮料</u>？
   茶
   酒

2. 您<u>喝红茶还是喝绿茶</u>？
   喝茶还是喝咖啡
   去北京饭店还是去马先生的公司
   是日本人还是韩国人

3. 林小姐喜欢<u>喝龙井</u>。
   喝绿茶
   喝红酒
   吃中国菜

4. 要<u>两瓶啤酒</u>。
   一杯茶
   两杯咖啡
   一瓶红酒

第二十一课　你们喝什么饮料？

1. 词的组合生成 The combination of *zi*-groups

我们把汉语中大于字、小于句的结构单位都叫词。词是由字组合生成的，根据结构特点，我们把汉语的词分为基本词、复合词和复杂词三类。

In this textbook, *zi*-group is defined as a structure unit larger than a *zi* and smaller than a sentence. The *zi*-group in Chinese is a kind of structure unit formed by *zi*. According to the structural characteristics, they are divided into three categories, namely, the basic *zi*-group, and the compound *zi*-group and the complex *zi*-group.

（1）**基本词**。由字与字直接组合生成的词叫基本词。例如：

The basic *zi*–group. It's directly formed of *zi*. For example:

  我们　　　　本子　　　　中国
  北京　　　　饭店　　　　学习
  汉语　　　　喜欢　　　　红酒

（2）**复合词**。由字与基本词组合生成，或者由基本词与基本词组合生成的词叫复合词。例如：

The compound *zi*-group. It's formed of a *zi* and a basic *zi*-group, or of two *zi*-groups. For example:

  我们的　　　　中国人
  北京饭店　　　学习汉语
  喜欢红酒　　　喝红酒

(3) **复杂词**。大于复合词的叫复杂词。例如:
The complex *zi*-group. *Zi*-groups larger than compound *zi*-groups are complex *zi*-groups. For example:

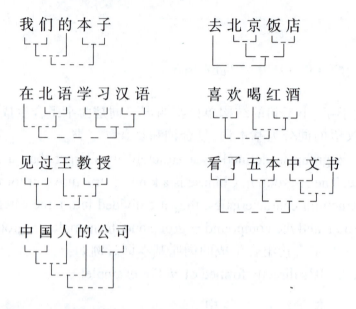

2. 字义例解和部件释义 Explanation of the meanings of *Hanzi* and *Hanzi* components

(1) 米。"米"的古字 ✳ 像一堆米,以米的形状代表米。象形字。"米"作部旁时写作"⺭"。

The ancient form of the *zi* for "米" resembles a pile of rice. It's a pictographic *zi*. When used as a left component, it's written as "⺭".

(2) 艹。"艹"的古字像两棵小草,以草的形状代表草。在现代汉字中只作部头和义符。带"艹部头"的汉字,其意思多半与花草等有关。

The ancient form of the *Hanzi* for "艹" (cǎo: grass) resembles two clusters of grass. The shape of grass stands for the grass. In modern Chinese it's only used as a top component. The meanings of *Hanzi* with this component are often related to flower, grass, etc.

(3) 菜。"菜"由"艹"和"采"组成。"艹"是义符,"采"是音符。形声字。"菜"的引申义为"菜肴"。

"菜" is composed of "艹" (cǎo: grass) and "采" (cǎi: pick). "艹" is the meaning component and "采" is the sound component. It's a picto-phonetic *zi*. Its extended meaning is "菜肴" (càiyáo: dishes).

(4) 井。"井"的古字 丼 像水井的形状,以水井的形状代表井。象形字。

第二十一课　你们喝什么饮料？

The ancient form of the *zi* for "井" resembles the shape of a well. The shape of water well stands for the well. It's a pictographic *zi*.

(5) 欠(qiàn: be short of)。"欠"的古字😀像人张大口吸气,表示体内氧气不足,意为欠缺。也用作部边和义符。有"欠"作部边的汉字,其意思多半与口的动作有关。指事字。

欠(qiàn: be short of). The ancient form of the *Hanzi* for "欠" resembles a person opening the mouth to draw deep breath. This means there is not enough oxygen in the body, meaning "lacking, being inadequate". It's also used as a right meaning component. The meanings of *Hanzi* with this component are often related to the action of the mouth. It's an indicative *zi*.

(6) 饮。"饮"由"饣"和"欠"组成,"饣"代表食品,"欠"代表嘴的动作。会意字。

饮 is composed of "饣"(shí: food) and "欠" (qiàn: be short of), the former indicates food and the latter the action of the mouth. It's an ideographic *zi*.

(7) 欢。"欢"是"歡"的简化字。"歡"由"雚"(guān)和"欠"组成,"欠"是义符,代表张口大笑(高兴)。"雚"是音符,作部旁时简化为"又"。

"欢" is the simplified form of the *Hanzi* for "歡", which is composed of "雚" (guān) and "欠" (qiàn: be short of). "欠" is the meaning component. It stands for laughing with the mouth open. "雚", as a left component, is simplified as "又" and is the sound component which shares the same final and tone with "欢".

(8) 酉。"酉"的古字🍶同"酒",像酒坛,以酒坛的形状代表酒。指事字。"酉"也作义符,有"酉"也作义符的汉字,其意思多半与酒类、其他发酵的食品及相关动作等有关。

The ancient form of the *Hanzi* for "酉" (yǒu: alcoholic beverage) is the same as "酒" (jiǔ: alcoholic beverage). It looks like a wine jug, which stands for wine. It's an indicative *zi*. The meanings of *Hanzi* with "酉" as a component are often related to wine, other barmy food or related action, etc.

3. 字词用法例解　Explanation of the usages of *zi* and *zi*-groups

呢。"呢"用在句尾表示疑问时有"在哪儿、怎么样、是不是"等意思。例如:

Interrogative particle *zi* "呢". "呢" coming at the end of a sentence means "where", "how", "yes / no". For example:

① 王太太呢？（王太太在哪儿？）
② 我身体很好,你呢？（我身体很好,你身体怎么样？）
③ 林正美会说汉语,三木呢？（林正美会说汉语,三木会不会说汉语？）
④ 马先生是中国人,马太太呢？（马先生是中国人,马太太是不是中国人？）

第二十二课
你们想吃什么菜?
Lesson Twenty-two
What Kind of Dish Would You Like?

一、部件 Components of *Hanzi*

1. 西部头 the *xī* top
   覀(要)(覀=西)
2. 冰部旁 the *bīng* left side
   冫(凉)(冰 *bīng* ice)(冫=冰)
3. 鸟部边 the *niǎo* right side
   鸟(鸭)(鸟 *niǎo* bird)
4. 斤部边 the *jīn* right side
   斤(斩)(斤 *jīn* unit of weight, = 0.5kg)

二、生字和生词 New *zi* and *zi*-groups

1.	烤 (kǎo)	roast; bake
2.	鸭 (yā)	duck
	烤鸭	roast duck
3.	只 (zhī)	*a measure-zi*
	一只鸭	one duck
4.	鱼 (yú)	fish
5.	条 (tiáo)	twig; a long narrow piece; *a measure-zi*
	一条鱼	one fish
6.	鲤 (lǐ)	carp
	鲤鱼	carp
7.	清 (qīng)	clear; explicit; distinct
8.	蒸 (zhēng)	steam
	清蒸	steam in clear soup (usu. without soy sauce)

9. 烧 (shāo) roast; braise; burn
   红烧 braise in soy sauce
10. 肉 (ròu) meat; pork
11. 豆 (dòu) pod-bearing plant or its seeds; bean
12. 腐 (fǔ) rotten; any bean product
    豆腐 (dòufu) bean curd
13. 青 (qīng) green; black; blue
    青菜 green vegetable
14. 热 (rè) be hot
    热菜 hot dish
15. 够 (gòu) enough; sufficient; adequate
16. 凉 (liáng) cool; cold
    凉菜 cold dish
17. 里 (lǐ) in; inside
    里面 inside; interior
    这里 (zhèli) 这儿
    那里 (nàli) 那儿
18. 斩 (zhǎn) chop; cut; kill
19. 鸡 (jī) chicken
    白斩鸡 tender boiled chicken with soy sauce

※　※　※　※　※

家常 the daily life of a family
家常豆腐 homely tofu

三、补充生词 Supplementary zi-groups

1. 烧烤 barbecue
2. 烧鸡 roast chicken
3. 青年 youth; young people
4. 凉快 (liángkuai) nice and cool
5. 天儿凉 it's cold
6. 天儿热 it's hot
7. 家常饭 homely food; simple meal
8. 家常菜 home cooking
9. 家常话 small talk; chitchat

四、唱读和口译 Read aloud and interpret

1. 菜
   白菜
   青菜
   热菜
   凉菜
   点菜
   吃菜
2. 烧
   烧鸡
   烧鸭
   烧烤
3. 红烧
   红烧肉
   红烧鱼
   红烧鲤鱼
   红烧豆腐
4. 烤
   烤鱼
   烤肉
   烤鸭
   北京烤鸭
5. 清蒸
   清蒸鸡
   清蒸鱼
   清蒸鲤鱼
6. 家常
   家常菜
   家常饭
   家常豆腐
   家常话

五、会话 Dialogue

你们想吃什么菜？

马太太：林小姐，请你点菜。

第二十二课 你们想吃什么菜?

林小姐:我不会点菜,您点。

马太太:林小姐太客气了,三木先生点吧。

三　木:马太太和马先生点。

马太太:你们想吃什么菜?

马先生:三木先生喜欢吃烤鸭,这里的烤鸭很好吃。

三　木:林小姐也喜欢吃烤鸭,她还喜欢吃鱼。

马太太:好。服务员,要一只烤鸭,一条鲤鱼。

服务员:好的。鲤鱼要清蒸的还是要红烧的?

马先生:红烧的好。这里的红烧肉和家常豆腐也很好吃,三木先生也都喜欢吃。马太太:好吧,要一条红烧鲤鱼,一个红烧肉,一个家常豆腐,再要一个青菜。

马　建:热菜够了,再要几个凉菜吧。这里的白斩鸡很好吃,林小姐最喜欢吃白斩鸡。

六、替换练习 Substitution drills

1. 请你<u>点菜</u>。
   说汉语
   这里坐
   去看王教授

2. <u>林小姐</u>太客气了。
   王太太
   你们
   大家

3. 你们喜欢<u>吃什么菜</u>?
   吃什么鱼
   喝什么茶
   喝什么酒

4. 这里的<u>红烧肉</u>很好吃。
   红烧豆腐
   红烧鲤鱼
   清蒸鲤鱼
   白斩鸡

45

烤鸭

5. 再要几个凉菜吧。
一个青菜
一个白斩鸡
几个凉菜
一条红烧鲤鱼
一瓶红酒

汉语知识
Chinese Language ABC

1. 词法结构（1）：限定结构　Zi-group structures (1): the restrictive structure

限定结构的词义特点是前面的字词说明后面的字词所代表的人或事物以及动作等的性质、特点等。例如：

Semantically, the restrictive structure means that the former *zi* or *zi*-group qualifies the latter *zi* or *zi*-group (a person, a thing, an action, etc.) in terms of nature, characteristics, etc. For example:

汉语	午饭	东面	电话号码	两个工人	马太太的儿子
好人	广场	红茶			
红烧	清蒸	红烧肉	清蒸鲤鱼		
飞机	烤鸭	饮料			
不说	没有	也去	很远	太大	

第二十二课 你们想吃什么菜？

2. 字义例解和部件释义 Explanation of the meanings of *Hanzi* and *Hanzi* components

（1）冫。"冫"的古字像水面冻结的冰纹，音和义与"冰"（bīng: ice）相同。"冫"在现代汉字中只作部旁，叫"冰部旁"，是义符。带冰部旁（冫）的汉字，其意思多半与寒冷、冻结等有关。

The ancient form of the *zi* for "冫" resembles lines on frozen water, its pronunciation and meaning are the same as "冰"（bīng: ice）. In modern *Hanzi*, it is called "冰部旁"（the ice side）and is used only as a left meaning component. *Zi* with "冫" is mostly related to cold or freezing.

（2）清。"清"由"冫"（水）和"青"组成，"冫"是义符，"青"是音符。"清"的意思是像水一样的清澈。形声字。

清 is formed of "冫"（水）（shuǐ: water）and "青"（qīng）, with "冫" being the meaning component and "青" the sound component. "清" means as clear as water. It's a picto-phonetic *zi*.

（3）烤。"烤"由"火"和"考"组成。"火"是义符，"考"是音符。形声字。

烤 is formed of "火" and "考"（kǎo）, with "火" being the meaning component and "考" the sound component. It's a picto-phonetic *zi*.

（4）鸟。"鸟"是"鳥"的简化字。"鳥"的古字像鸟的形状，以鸟的形状代表"鸟"。象形字。有"鸟"作义符的汉字，其意思多半与鸟类有关。

鸟（niǎo: bird）is the simplified form of "鳥". The ancient form of "鳥" resembles the shape of a bird. It's a pictographic *zi*. *Zi* with "鸟" as the meaning component is mostly related to bird.

（5）鸡。"鸡"是"鷄"的简化字。"鷄"由"奚"（xī）和"鳥"组成，"鳥"是义符，"奚"是音符（近似音）。"奚"作部旁时简化为"又"。

鸡 is the simplified form of "鷄," formed of "奚"（xī）and "鳥"（niǎo: bird）, with "鳥" being the meaning component and "奚", approximately, the sound component. As a left component, "奚" is simplified as "又".

（6）鸭。"鸭"由"甲"和"鸟"组成，"甲"是音符（近似音），"鸟"是义符。

鸭 is formed of "甲"（jiǎ）and "鸟"（niǎo: bird）, with "甲", approximately, being the sound component, and "鸟" the meaning component.

（7）鱼。"鱼"是"魚"的简化字。"魚"的古字像鱼的形状，以鱼的形状代表"鱼"。象形字。

鱼 is the simplified form of "魚". The ancient form of "魚" resembles the shape of a fish. It's a pictographic *zi*.

（8）鲤。"鲤"由"鱼"和"里"组成，"鱼"是义符，"里"是音符。形声字。

鲤 is formed of "鱼" and "里", with "鱼" being the meaning component and "里" the sound component. It's a picto-phonetic zi.

3. 字词用法例解 Explanation of the usages of zi and zi-groups

(1) 吧。"吧"可以用于表示协商、赞同、确认、估量等语气。例如：
"吧" can be used to show a tone of consulting, agreement, confirmation, assessment, etc. For example:

A：马先生办公室的电话没人接。(No one answers the phone in Mr. Ma's office.)
B：你打他的手机吧。(You can phone his mobile.)
A：我们去看王先生，你也去吧。(I hope you will also join us to visit Mr. Wang.)
B：好吧。(I agree to see Mr. Wang.)
A：我们去哪儿吃饭？(Where will we have a meal?)
B：去北京饭店吧。(My suggestion is that we go to Beijing Hotel for meal.)
A：去北京饭店多长时间能到？(How long can we get Beijing Hotel?)
B：二十分钟吧。(It takes about twenty minutes.)
A：什么时候吃午饭？(When will we have lunch?)
B：十二点吧。(It's probably around twelve o'clock when we will have lunch.)
A：你去过王先生家吧？(I guess you have been to Mr. Wang's home.)
B：没有，我没去过王先生家。(No, I have't been to Mr. Wang's home.)

(2) 好的。"好的"用于答复对方的要求，是同意的意思。
"好的" is used as a reply to one's requirement and means agreement.

(3) 红烧的。这里的"红烧的"是"红烧的鲤鱼"的意思。
"红烧的" here means "红烧的鲤鱼".

第二十三课
你们要什么主食？

Lesson Twenty-three
What Staple Food Would You Like?

一、部件 Components of *Hanzi*

1. 小部头 the xiǎo top
   ⺌（尝）(⺌ = 小)
2. 方部底 the fāng bottom
   ⽅（方）(⽅ 音 fāng)
3. 玉部旁 the yù left side
   王（现）(王 = 玉)(玉 yù jade)
4. 包部框 the bāo frame
   勹（包）(勹 音 bāo)

二、生字和生词 New *zi* and *zi*-groups

1. 主 (zhǔ)   host; owner; be in charge of; preside over
   主人   host; master; owner
   做主   decide; have the final say
2. 食 (shí)   food; meal; eat
   主食   staple food; principal food
   饭食   food
   饮食   food and drink; diet
3. 已 (yǐ)   already
   已经   already
4. 饱 (bǎo)   have eaten to the full
   饱了   be full; have eaten to the full

吃饱	have eaten one's fill
吃饱了	饱了
5. 饺 (jiǎo)	a kind of dumpling
饺子 (jiǎozi)	dumpling (with meat and vegetable stuffing)
6. 斤 (jīn)	*a unit of weight, equivalent to 0.5 kilogram*
7. 尝 (cháng)	taste; have a taste of
尝尝 (chángchang)	have a taste of
8. 碗 (wǎn)	bowl; bowl-like vessel or object; *a measure-zi*
一个碗	one bowl
一碗	one bowl of
9. 米 (mǐ)	rice; shelled or husked seed (usu. edible)
大米	rice
米饭	cooked rice
一碗米饭	one bowl of cooked rice
10. 方 (fāng)	direction; square; place
南方	south; the South
东方	east; the East; the Orient
西方	west; the West
北方	north; the North
11. 数 (shù)	number; figure
多数	majority; major
12. 面 (miàn)	wheat flour
面食	food made from flour
面条	noodle
13. 前 (qián)	front; before
前天	the day before yesterday
前年	year before last
以前	before; previous
14. 现 (xiàn)	show; appear; reveal
现在	now; nowadays; currently
15. 包 (bāo)	wrap; bag
包子 (bāozi)	steamed stuffed bun
面包	bread
书包	schoolbag
打包	ale; pack
16. 爱 (ài)	like; love; be fond of; keen on

第二十三课　你们要什么主食？

爱吃	like eating
爱人 (àiren)	husband or wife
17. 叫 (jiào)	order
18. 心 (xīn)	heart
好心	kind-hearted
小心	careful
点心 (diǎnxin)	refreshments

三、补充生词　Supplementary *zi*-groups

1. 经过　　　　　pass; through; process
2. 主体　　　　　main body; main or principal part
3. 主要　　　　　main; major; principal
4. 方面　　　　　aspect
5. 方向　　　　　direction; orientation
6. 前方　　　　　ahead; in front
7. 前面　　　　　in front; forward
8. 向前　　　　　ahead; forward
9. 向前看　　　　look forward
10. 数字　　　　　numeral; figure
11. 实现　　　　　realize; achieve; bring about
12. 爱国　　　　　love one's country; be patriotic
13. 爱好 (àihào)　take great pleasure in
14. 爱美　　　　　set great store by one's appearance
15. 爱面子　　　　be concerned about face-saving
16. 有心　　　　　have a mind to; intentionally; purposely
17. 有心人　　　　person who is resolved to do sth. useful; observant and conscientious person

四、唱读和口译　Read aloud and interpret

1. 子 (zi)
   包子
   儿子
   饺子
   里子 (lining)
   面子

2. 尝尝
   吃吃
   说说
   想想
   叫叫
   看看
   问问
3. 南方人
   北方人
   东方人
   西方人

五、会话 Dialogue

你们要什么主食？

马太太：你们要什么主食？
林小姐：我已经吃饱了。
马太太：这儿的饺子很好吃，林小姐也尝尝。
马先生：再要一碗米饭，我太太是南方人，她喜欢吃米饭。
三　木：南方人都喜欢吃米饭吗？
马先生：多数南方人喜欢吃米饭，多数北方人喜欢吃面食。
马太太：我以前不喜欢吃面食，现在也喜欢了，面条、包子、饺子我都爱吃。
马　建：我好久没吃面条了。
马太太：好，再要一碗面条。
马先生：要不要叫点心？
三　木：不要了吧，都已经吃饱了。

六、替换练习 Substitution drills

1. 你们要什么<u>主食</u>？
   饮料
   茶
   酒
2. 要不要<u>叫点心</u>？
   请王教授
   去看王太太

3. 我已经吃饱了。
   看见马阳
   来到北京饭店

4. 这里的饺子很好吃，<u>林小姐也尝尝</u>。
   马太太也尝尝
   你们也尝尝
   大家都尝尝

5. 我以前不喜欢吃面食，现在也喜欢了。
   吃米饭
   吃豆腐
   坐飞机
   坐公共汽车
   打的

1. 词法结构 (2)：动受结构　Zi-group structures (2): the action-recipient structure

　　代表动作接受者或相关者的词语可以放在动字后面组成动受结构。动受结构的词义特点是动字后面的字词代表动作的对象、内容、方位、处所等。例如：

　　The action-recipient structure is formed of an action-*zi* and *zi*-groups that stand for the recipient or other related *zi*-groups, denoting the receiver of the action or other relevant person or thing. The semantic feature of this kind of structure is that the *zi* or *zi*-group following the action-*zi* indicates the receiver, content, direction, location, etc. of the action. For example:

打 的
└──

吃 饭
└──

喝 绿茶
└──

姓 王
└──

叫 王同
└─┘─

向 东
└─┘─

在 家
└─┘

去 北京饭店
└─┘──

2. 字义例解和部件释义 Explanation of the meanings of *Hanzi* and *Hanzi* components

(1) 勹。"勹"的古字⌒像人弯着腰伸开双臂裹物的样子,以此代表"包"。"勹"在现代汉字中只作部框。

The ancient form of the *zi* for "勹" is like a person bending over with the arms extended to hold something to the bosom. This stands for bundling. In modern Chinese "勹" is just used as a component.

(2) 包。包由"勹"和"巳"(sì)组成,"巳"的古字像胎儿的形状,"包"像胎儿被包着,以胎儿被包着的样子代表"包"。"勹"也是音符。会意兼形声字。

"包" is composed of "勹" (bāo: wrap; bundle) and "巳" (sì). The ancient form of the *zi* for "巳" is like a foetus. "包" resembles a foetus being wrapped up, which means wrapping up. "勹" is also the sound component. It's not only a self-explanatory *zi* but also an ideographic *zi*.

(3) 石。"石"的古字像山石的形状,以山石的形状代表"石"。象形字。

The ancient form of the *zi* for "石" resembles the shape of a rock, which stands for "石". It's a pictographic *zi*.

(4) 碗。"碗"由"石"和"宛"组成,最初的碗是石制品,所以用"石"作义符。"宛"是音符。形声字。

"碗" is composed of "石" (shí: stone; rock) and "宛" (wǎn). Bowl was originally made of stone. "石" is the meaning component, and "宛" the sound component. It's a picto-phonetic *zi*.

(5) 饺。"饺"由"饣"和"交"组成,"饣"是义符,"交"是音符。形声字("饺"和"交"声调不同)。

"饺" is composed of "饣" and "交" (jiāo: hand over; cross), with "饣" being the meaning component and "交" the sound component. It's a picto-phonetic *zi*. ("饺" and "交" have different tones)

(6) 饱。"饱"由"饣"和"包"组成,"饣"是形符,"包"是音符。形声字("饱"和"包"的声调不同)。

"饱"(bǎo: have eaten one's fill; be full) is composed of "饣" (shí: food) and "包" (bāo: wrap; bag), with "饣" being the meaning component and "包" the sound component. It's a picto-phonetic zi ("饱" and "包" have different tones)

(7) 王。"王"是"玉"作部旁时的变体。"玉"的古字 像一串玉。象形字。

"王"(yù: jade) is the variant of "玉"(yù: jade) when used as a left component. The ancient form of the zi for "玉" is like a string of jade and it's a pictographic zi.

(8) 现。"现"由王(玉)和"见"组成,以玉可见表示玉的出现,泛指出现。会意字。

"现"(xiàn: appear) is composed of "王"(yù: jade) and "见"(jiàn: see). The visible jade indicates the appearance of jade. It's extended to the meaning of appearance. It's an ideographic zi.

3. 字词用法例解 Explanation of the usages of zi and zi-groups

(1) 动字重叠。有些动字可以重叠,生成重叠式动词。重叠式动词的词义特点是表示轻松地做。后面的动字一般读轻声。例如:

Reduplication of action-zi. Some action-zi can be reduplicated. One of the meanings of the reduplicated action-zi is to indicate that the action is done in a relaxed and easy way. The second syllable of an action-zi of this kind is often pronounced in the neutral tone. For example:

说说　尝尝　想想　看看

这类动字也可以加"一"后再重叠,表示动作不重或动作的时间不长。例如:

"一" can be inserted between the two syllables of the reduplicated action-zi, implying that the action will not last long. For example:

说一说　尝一尝　想一想　看一看

(2) "南方"和"北方"。在中国,南方一般是指长江流域及其以南地区,北方一般是指黄河流域及其以北地区。

"南方" and "北方". In China "南方" normally refers to the area south of and to the Yangtze River. "北方" normally refers to the area north of and to the Yellow River.

(3) **名字用作量字**。有不少量字是由名字充当的,例如:
Nominal-*zi* used as measure-*zi*. Some nominal-*zi* can act as measure-*zi*. For example:

一个碗;一碗米饭。

一个杯子;一杯茶,一杯啤酒。

一个酒瓶;一瓶啤酒,一瓶红酒。

第二十四课
共计九百零二元

Lesson Twenty-four Altogether 902 Yuan

一、部件 Components of *Hanzi*

1. 彳部旁 the chì left side
   彳(得)（彳 chì walk）
2. 戈部边 the gē right side
   戈(找)（戈 gē dagger-axe）
3. 尤部边 the Yóu right side
   尤(优)（尤 yóu fault; remarkable）
4. 戋部边 the Jiān right side
   戋(钱)（戋 jiān）
5. 攵部边 the pū right side
   攵(做)（攵=攴）（攴 pū beat, strike）

二、生字和生词 New *zi* and *zi*-groups

1. 计 (jì)   count; calculate
   共计   add up to; amount to
2. 百 (bǎi)   hundred
3. 元 (yuán)   unit of money
4. 零 (líng)   zero
5. 得 (de)   *a structural particle*
   吃得太多   to have eaten too much
6. 少 (shǎo)   be few; be little
   很少   be very little
   不少   be not so few; considerable; ample
   多少 (duōshao)   how many; how much
7. 结 (jié)   settle; finish; conclude

57

8.	账 (zhàng)	account; account book
	结账	settle accounts; square accounts; balance the books
9.	钱 (qián)	money; cash; coin
	多少钱	how much
10.	单 (dān)	bill; list; single
	账单	bill; account; check
	菜单	menu
	名单	name list
11.	优 (yōu)	good; excellent
	优先	have priority; take precedence; have precedence
12.	惠 (huì)	favor; kindness; benefit
	优惠	preferential; favorable
13.	折 (zhé)	discount; rebate
	打折	sell at a discount; give a discount
	八折	80% of the original price; 20% discount
	打八折	charge 80% of the original price; give 20% discount
14.	买 (mǎi)	buy; purchase
	买单	pay for the bill
	买东西	buy things
15.	千 (qiān)	thousand
16.	找 (zhǎo)	look for; hunt for; try to discover
	找人	look for sb
	找东西	look for sth.
	找工作	look for a job
	找钱	give change
17.	餐 (cān)	food; meal
	中餐	Chinese cuisine; Chinese food
	西餐	Western-style food; Western food
	餐饮	food and drink
18.	宜 (yí)	suitable; appropriate; desirable
	便宜 (piányi)	cheap; inexpensive
19.	次 (cì)	time
	下次	next time
	上次	last time

※ ※ ※ ※ ※

	下回	下次
	做东	act as host to sb.

三、补充生词 Supplementary *zi*-groups

1. 钱包   wallet; purse
2. 有钱人   the rich; the wealthy
3. 韩元   Korean won
4. 美元   US dollar; American dollar
5. 日元   Japanese yen
6. 单位   unit
7. 就餐   *formal* dine; have a meal
8. 次数   number of times; frequency

四、唱读和口译 Read aloud and interpret

1. 共计
   共计五十二(52)人
   共计八百(800)元
   共计七百九十(790)元
   共计两千二百二十(2220)元
   共计两千二百二十二(2222)元
   共计四千五百一十六(4516)元
   共计三千零二十一元(3021)(零 líng: zero)

2. 得
   吃得太多
   吃得不少
   吃得很好
   说得很好
   说得不好
   走得太快
   看得不快
   买得不少

3. 钱
   有钱
   没(有)钱
   给钱
   钱很多
   钱太少

五、会话 Dialogue

共计九百零二元

马太太：大家都吃饱了吗?
三　木：吃饱了。
林小姐：我吃得太多了。
马　建：林小姐吃得很少。
马太太：结账吧。
马　建：服务员,结账。多少钱?
服务员：这是账单,共计九百零二元。
马太太：有优惠吗?
服务员：打过八折了。
马　建：我来买单。这是一千元。
服务员：给您找钱,找您九十八元。
林小姐：谢谢买单的。
马　建：这是我妈给我的钱,我妈的钱比我多。
马太太：中餐很便宜,下次请你们吃西餐。
三　木：下回我做东。

六、替换练习 Substitution drills

1. 有优惠吗? ——打过八折了。
   打八折
   八折优惠

2. 给您找钱,找您九十二元。
   找您五十八元
   找您二十六元

3. 中餐很便宜。
   中餐 不贵
   西餐 很贵
   西餐 不便宜
   烤鸭 很便宜
   龙井茶 不便宜

4. 我妈的钱比我(的钱)多。
   (1) 马太太的钱比马先生(的钱)多。
   　　马先生的钱没有马太太(的钱)多。
   (2) 中国比美国人多。

美国没有中国人多。
(3) 中国比英国大。
英国没有中国大。
(4) 马建比马阳大。
马阳没有马建大。
(5) 马阳比马建高。
马建没有马阳高。

5. 下次请你们吃西餐。
吃烤鸭
去我家吃饭
去我家喝茶
来这里喝咖啡

6. 下回我做东。
今天我做东
下回三木做东
林正美也要做东

1. 词法结构（3）：表示动作结果的动补结构 Zi-group structures（3）: the action-complement structure showing the result of an action

要说明某动作产生什么结果，可以在表示动作的字词后面加上说明动作结果的字词。由表示动作的字词和说明动作结果的字词组成的结构单位叫动补结构。这类动补结构的组成方式有：

A zi or zi-group following an action-zi can show the result of the action. Then such a structure is called the action-complement structure. This kind of structure is formed in the following ways:

(1) 表示动作的字词+表示动作的字词——"动动式"动补结构。例如：
The action-complement structure is formed of "action-zi + action-zi". For example:
① 看见

② 想到
③ 走到

(2) 表示动作的字词+表示状况的字词——"动静式"动补结构。例如：

The action-complement structure is formed of "action-*zi* + descriptive *zi*". For example:

① 吃饱
② 走近
③ 想好

"动动式"和"动静式"动补结构的肯定式是在动补结构后面加"了"，否定式是在动补结构前面加"没(有)"。例如：

"了" following either of the above two action-complement structures is to show affirmation, while "没(有)" preceding "了" indicates negation. For example:

① 看见　看见了　没(有)看见
② 想到　想到了　没(有)想到
③ 吃饱　吃饱了　没(有)吃饱

(3) 表示动作的字词+得+表示状况的字词——"动得静"动补结构。例如：

The action-complement structure is formed of "action-*zi* + 得 + the descriptive *zi*". For example:

① 吃得太多　eat too much
② 学得很快　learn sth. quickly
③ 说得很好　speak very well

如果要指出"动得静"动补结构中动作的对象、内容等，可以用"动受 + 动补"。例如：

To indicate specifically the receiver, content, etc. of the action, the pattern "action-recipient+action-complement" is used. For example:

① 吃烤鸭吃得太多 eat too much roast duck
② 学汉语学得很快 learn Chinese quickly
③ 说英语说得很好 speak English very well

"动补结构"和"动受动补结构"的肯定式是在后面加"了"。例如：

The affirmative form of both the action-complement structure and the "action-recipient+action-complement" structure is to add "了" after them.

① 吃得太多了　have eaten too much
　　吃烤鸭吃得太多了 have eaten too much roast duck
② 学得很快了　learn sth. quickly
　　学汉语学得很快了 learn Chinese quickly

第二十四课　共计九百零二元

③ 说得很好了 speak very well now

　　说英语说得很好了 speak English very well now

"动补结构"和"动受动补结构"的否定式是在"得"的后面加"不"。例如：
The negative form is to use "不" after "得". For example:

① 吃得不多 eat not too much

　　吃烤鸭吃得不多 eat not too much roasted duck

② 学得不快 learn not too quick

　　学汉语学得不快 learn Chinese not so quick

③ 说得不好 speak not so well

　　说英语说得不好 speak English not so well

2. 字义例解和部件释义 Explanation of the meanings of *Hanzi* and *Hanzi* components

(1) 戈。"戈"的古字像一种兵器，以这种兵器的形状代表兵器。象形字。

The ancient form of the *zi* for "戈" (gē: dagger-axe) is like a kind of weapon. The shape of the weapon represents arms. It's a pictographic *zi*.

(2) 攵。"攵"是"攴"的变体，"攴"的古字像手持棍棒扑击。带"攵"的汉字多半是动字。

"攵" (pū: rush at) is the variant of "攴" (pū: beat; strike). The ancient form of the *Hanzi* for "攴" resembles flapping with stick in hand. *Hanzi* with "攵" as a component are mostly action-*zi*.

(3) 少。在"小"字下面加"丿"，表示数量小。指事字。

"丿" added at the bottom of the *zi* "小" shows the small number. It's an indicative *zi*.

(4) 千。"千"由"一"和"十"构成。"一"在这里代表"百"，"一"与"十"组合，表示是"一百个十"，即百乘以十，等于千。指事字。

"千" (qiān: thousand) is composed of "一" and "十". "一" here stands for "百" (bǎi: hundred). The combination of "一" and "百" means "one hundred tens", that's to multiply one hundred by ten, equal to one thousand. It's an indicative *zi*.

(5) 钱。"钱"由"钅"和"戋"组成。古代钱币用金属制成，所以用"钅"作义符。"戋"是音符(韵母相近)。形声字。

"钱" is composed of "钅" (jīn: gold) and "戋" (jiān). In ancient times, coins were made of gold. Therefore "钅" is used as the meaning component and "戋" the sound component. It's a picto phonetic *zi*.

(6) 优。"优"由"亻"和"尤"组成，"亻"是义符，"尤"是音符("优"和"尤"声调不同)。形声字。

"优" is composed of "亻" and "尤", of which "亻" is the meaning component and "尤" the sound component ("优" and "尤" differ in tones). It's a picto-phonetic *zi*.

(7) 彳。"彳"的古字意为小步行走,在现代汉字中也用作部旁。有"彳"作部旁的汉字,其意思多与行走、行动等有关。

The ancient form of the *Hanzi* for "彳" (chì) means walking slowly. It's also used as a left component in modern *Hanzi*. Meanings of *Hanzi* with "彳" are often related to walking, action, etc.

3. 字词用法例解 Explanation of the usages of *zi* and *zi*-groups

(1) 货币单位。中国的货币单位从小到大有:分(fēn)、角(jiǎo)、元(yuán)。1元＝10角,1角＝10分。在口语中,"角"也说"毛"(máo),"元"也说"块"(kuài)。

Currency units. The currency units in China from small to large are 分(fēn), 角(jiǎo) and 元(yuán). 1 元 equals to 10 角, and 1 角 equals to 10 分. In spoken Chinese, "角" can be said as "毛" (máo) and "元" "块" (kuài).

(2) 下次、下回。"下次"和"下回"意思相同,"下回"多用于口语。

"下次" has the same meaning as "下回" which is often used in spoken Chinese.

第二十五课　复习（五）
Lesson Twenty-five　Review (5)

一、说出下列部件的名称 Tell the names of the following *Hanzi* components

1. 艹（茶）
2. 宀（方）
3. 宀（实）
4. 小（尝）
5. 西（要）
6. 灬（蒸）
7. 刀（方）
8. 心（惠）
9. 采（菜）
10. 氵（酒）
11. 冫（凉）
12. 王（现）
13. 饣（饮）
14. 纟（红）
15. 火（烤）
16. 讠（计）
17. 扌（折）
18. 车（斩）
19. 米（料）
20. 鱼（鲤）
21. 攵（做）
22. 戈（钱）
23. 欠（欢）
24. 酉（酒）
25. 鸟（鸭）
26. 斤（斩）
27. 戈（找）
28. 青（清）
29. 里（鲤）
30. 见（现）
31. 工（红）
32. 多（够）
33. 包（饱）
34. 非（啡）
35. 尤（优）
36. 囗（回）
37. 勺（包）
38. 广（腐）
39. 玉（国）
40. 斤（近）
41. 口（可）

二、朗读下列汉字，并说出每个汉字的义符 Read aloud the following *Hanzi* and tell the names of the meaning components

喝　欢　饱　饮　饺　餐　菜　茶　烧　烤　点
热　蒸　酒　凉　鸡　鸭　鲤　现　碗　钱　接
折　叫　做

三、朗读下列汉字，并说出每个汉字的音符 Read aloud the following *Hanzi* and tell the names of the sound components

清　请　鲤　饱　现　码　妈　吗　饺　较　汽　钟

65

四、朗读下列词语，体会词语的构成方式和词义结构 Read aloud the following zi-groups and make clear their form and semantic structures

1. 名词

   (1) 北京　北京人　北京大学　北京饭店　北京烤鸭　本人　本身　本书　父亲　母亲　师母　汉语　汉字　红酒　绿茶　青菜　青年　时间　今年　龙井　工人　客人　友人　主人　主食　主体　早饭　午饭(中饭)　晚饭　老年人　书本　知识　大学教授　公司经理　广场前面

   (2) 电话　电子　汽车　天气　海上　上海　龙井茶　里面　南方　手机　上午　上次　下午　下次　文人　文本　文学　美元　西餐　中餐　中国

   (3) 车站　饭店　书店　钱包　书包　账单　名单　名字　名次　数字　号码　电话号码

   (4) 父母　子女　饭菜　饮食　朋友　方面　时候

   (5) 人口　身体　国家

   (6) 米饭　面食　肉食

   (7) 大学　大米　小姐　小姐姐　好人　女人　老人　忙人　大忙人　老朋友　喜面　广场　小说　凉菜　热菜　青菜　白酒　红茶　多数　少数　早上　早日　专业　家常菜　总经理　有钱人　有心人

   (8) 大家　大门　大人　小人　小姐　白天

   (9) 烤鸭　烧鸡　白斩鸡　清蒸鱼　红烧肉

   (10) 教授　经理　总理　爱好　关系　知识　现在

   (11) 白菜　鲤鱼　东西　豆腐

2. 动词

   (1) 介绍　认识　比较　辅导　服务　喜欢　欢喜　学习　离开　应该　教授　经理　爱好　关系　总理

   (2) 吃饭　喝茶　看书　请客　祝寿　打的　学习汉语　认识马阳　辅导英语

   (3) 红烧　清蒸　白斩　远走　高飞　公共　专有　实习　多谢　幸会

   (4) 会说　能到　敢想　过奖　共计　经过　请问

   (5) 见到　见过　去过　看见　住在

   (6) 回来　上去　过去　向前　向前看

   (7) 吃饱　说明　问好　问安

   (8) 看见一个人　走到那里　去过南京　吃饱晚饭

   (9) 打折　教学　爱吃　爱美

   (10) 面向　八折　小心

3. 静词(形容词)

友好　家常　有钱　有心　健康　快乐　广大　远大
长久　共同　好吃

4. "动得静"结构

(1) 吃得很饱　走得很累　飞得太远　买得不多
(2) 吃得很多　走得很快　说得不好　看得不远

五、朗读下列常用语句 Read aloud the following frequently used sentences

1. 服务员,点菜。
2. 林小姐,请你点菜。
3. 你们喝什么饮料?
4. 来两瓶啤酒。
5. 要一只烤鸭。
6. 再要几个凉菜吧。
7. 你们要什么主食?
8. 要不要叫点心?
9. 我已经吃饱了。
10. 这是账单,共计九百八十五元。
11. 有优惠吗?
12. 八折优惠。
13. 打八折。
14. 打过八折了。
15. 下回我做东。

六、说话练习 Oral practice

表演在饭店请客吃饭,按下列程序会话:

1. 点菜问答
   (1) 喝什么饮料
   (2) 喜欢吃什么菜
   (3) 要什么主食
   (4) 还要喝什么、吃什么

2. 结账问答
   (1) 共计多少钱

(2) 有没有优惠,优惠多少
(3) 给多少钱,找多少钱

3. 争取(zhēngqǔ: win over)做东
(1) 下回谁做东
(2) 下回在哪儿、吃什么

七、说快板儿 Read and recite a clapper talk

口手歌

The mouth and the hand (a rhyme)

吃有口,喝有口,
说有口,唱有口,
骂字头上两个口。

打有手,用有手。
举有手,看有手,
手挽手,是好友。

生字

1. 唱 (chàng)   sing
2. 骂 (mà)   call names; curse
3. 举 (jǔ)   lift; raise
4. 挽 (wǎn)   draw; pull

第二十六课 马总正在开会
Lesson Twenty-six
General Manager Ma is at a Meeting

一、部件 Components of *Hanzi*

1. 竹部头 the zhú top
   ⺮（等）(⺮ = 竹)(竹 zhú bamboo)
2. 足部旁 the zú left side
   ⻊（路）(⻊ = 足)(足 zú foot)
3. 予部旁 the yǔ left side
   予（预）(予 yǔ give; grant)
4. 页部边 the yè right side
   页（顺）(页 yè page; head)

二、生字和生词 New *zi* and *zi*-groups

1. 开 (kāi)   open; start; operate; boil
   开门   open the door
   开学   school opens; term begins
   开车   drive a car
2. 会 (huì)   meeting; party; association; society
   开会   hold or attend a meeting
   会客   receive a visitor or guest
   会客室   reception room
   晚会   evening party
3. 迎 (yíng)   meet; greet; welcome
   欢迎   welcome
   迎接   receive; meet; greet
4. 预 (yù)   in advance; beforehand
   预先   in advance; beforehand

5. 约 (yuē) agree; make an appointment; arrange
   约会 make an appointment; make an arrangement to meet
   约好 make an appointment in advance
   预约 预先约好
7. 路 (lù) road; way
   马路 road; pavement
   公路 highway
   路上 on the road
   路过 pass by or through (a place)
   过路 pass by one's way
8. 顺 (shùn) agreeable; obey; yield to
   顺路 on the way; direct route
   不顺 not so smooth
9. 便 (biàn) convenient; handy; informal
   方便 convenient
   顺便 incidentally; in passing
10. 对 (duì) correct; right; treat; be directed at
    不对 incorrect
11. 起 rise; *up to a certain standard*
    起来 rise; stand up; sit up
    起名字 give a name
    对得起 treat fairly; do justice to
    对不起 sorry; excuse me
    看得起 have a good opinion of; think highly of
    看不起 look down upon
    买得起 can afford to buy
    买不起 can't afford to buy
12. 等 (děng) wait; and so on
    等人 wait for a person
    等一会儿 wait a minute
13. 题 (tí) topic; write; inscribe
    问题 problem; question
    没问题 no problem
14. 真 (zhēn) true; real; really; indeed
    真的 real; true
    真快 really fast

真正	real; genuine; really
15. 水 (shuǐ)	water
开水	boiled water
水不开	the water is not boiled
水开了	the water is boiled
水没开	the water has not been boiled
16. 必 (bì)	certainly; surely; necessarily
不必	not necessarily
17. 周 (zhōu)	Zhou (*a surname*); week; circumference; circle
两周	two weeks
周到	thoughtful; considerate
18. 男 (nán)	man; male
男人	man
男的	男人
男朋友	boyfriend
19. 秘 (mì)	secret; confidential; keep sth. secret
秘书	secretary
20. 为 (wéi)	do; act; be; mean
以为	think; consider
认为	think; consider

※　　　※　　　※　　　※　　　※

马总	马飞总经理
正在	in process of

三、补充生词 Supplementary *zi*-groups

1. 条约　　　treaty; pact
2. 走路　　　walk; go on foot
3. 路面　　　road surface; pavement
4. 一起　　　together
5. 和……一起　together with
6. 题字　　　write; inscribe
7. 不便　　　不方便
8. 小便　　　urinate; piss
9. 大便　　　human excrement; shit

四、唱读和口译 Read aloud and interpret

1. 路
   马路
   公路
   大路
   小路
2. 过
   路过
   经过
   走过
   飞过
3. 正在
   正在开会
   正在会客
   正在吃饭
   正在打电话
   正在买东西
4. 您请……
   您请坐
   您请里面坐
   您请这儿坐
   您请那儿坐
   您请喝水
   您请喝茶
   您请喝酒
   您请吃菜
5. 会
   会说汉语
   会写汉字（写 xiě: write）
   开会
   会客
   会客室
   不会有人接电话
   最近不会去上海
   等一会儿
   一会儿就来

第二十六课　马总正在开会

五、会话 Dialogue

马总正在开会

三木：小姐,总经理在吗?
秘书：您是……?
三木：我叫三木,是马总的朋友。
秘书：欢迎! 您预约过吗?
三木：没有。我路过这里,顺便来看看马总。
秘书：对不起,马总正在开会,您能等等吗?
三木：没问题,我等一会儿。
秘书：您汉语说得真好,是在哪儿学的?
三木：过奖! 我是在北京语言大学学的。
秘书：会客室在里面,您请里面坐。您请喝水。
三木：谢谢! 小姐贵姓?
秘书：免贵姓周。我叫周男,是总经理办公室的秘书,您就叫我小周吧。
三木：周秘书是南方人吗?
周男：对,我是南京人。不过我的名字是"男女"的"男",不是"南方"的"南"。
三木：是吗? 我还以为是"南方"的"南"呢。这个名字真好。

六、替换练习 Substitution drills

1. 马总<u>正在开会</u>。
   正在会客
   正在办公
   正在吃饭
   正在喝咖啡

2. 马太太<u>正在吃饭呢</u>。
   正在看书呢
   正在打电话呢

3. 林小姐<u>在买东西呢</u>。
   在说话呢
   在学汉语呢

4. 我路过这里,顺便来看看马总。
   顺便来看看大家
   顺便买点东西
5. 这个名字真好。
   这里的烤鸭
   他的英语
   你说汉语说得

1. 句法结构(1):主体和述体 Sentence structure(1): the topic and the comment

汉语的基本句一般由主体和述体两部分组成。主体在前,代表"谁"或"什么";述体在后,用来说明它的主体"做什么"或者"怎么样"。由此可见,汉语基本句的语义结构模式就是"谁(什么)——做什么(怎么样)"。例如:

A Chinese basic sentence is normally composed of two parts: the topic and the comment. The topic, indicating "who" or "what", is followed by the comment which explains what the topic does, or how it is. Therefore, the semantic structure of a basic sentence may be understood as "who(what)——do what(how)". For example:

① 我家｜四口人。
② 马先生｜是中国人。
③ 他｜姓王。
④ 王师母｜没有手机。
⑤ 马先生家｜在长安街。
⑥ 他们｜去北京饭店吃饭。
⑦ 林小姐｜喜欢喝龙井。
⑧ 王教授｜身体不太好。
⑨ 龙井茶｜很有名。

上面的例句,竖线前面的是主体,竖线后面的是述体。

In the sentences above, the part before the vertical line is the topic, and the part after the vertical line is the comment.

表示时间、地点、方位、数量等的字词也可以担任主体,作为述体陈述的对象。例如:

Zi or *zi*-groups of time, place, locality, number, etc, can serve as the topic that is talked about. For example:

① 今天｜星期六。
② 十二点｜吃午饭。
③ 有的时候｜上街买东西。
④ 天安门广场｜在长安街。
⑤ 北京饭店｜远不远?
⑥ 这儿｜没有饭店。
⑦ 东面｜有很多人。
⑧ 三十｜就是三个十。

在语境清楚(有上下文)的情况下,基本句可以不出现主体或述体。例如:

When the context is clear, the topic or the comment of a basic sentence can be omitted. For example:

① ｜要一条鱼。
② ｜二十分钟吧。
③ ｜够了。
④ (谁请你吃饭?)马太太｜。
⑤ (谁在等马总?)三木｜。

在上面的例子中,例①～例③未出现主体;例④和例⑤未出现述体。

In the sentences above, the topics in 1, 2 and 3 are omitted, while in 4 and 5 the comments are left out.

2. 字义例解和部件释义　Explanation of the meanings of *Hanzi* and *Hanzi* components

(1) ⺮。"⺮"是"竹"作部头时的变体。"竹"的古字帅像两支竹叶。以"⺮"作部头的汉字,其意思多半与"竹"或竹制品有关。

"⺮", a top component, is the variant of "竹". The ancient form of the *zi* for "竹" is like two bamboo leaves. The meanings of *Hanzi* with this component are often related to bamboo or products originally made of bamboo.

(2) 等。由"⺮"(zhú: bamboo)和"寺"(sì: temple)组成。"⺮"代表竹制品。中国古代用竹制品计数、算数和刻写文字。中国古代的"寺"是执法机构。由"⺮"和"寺"组成"等",表示由执法机构通过计算和制定法律来达到均等。会意字。用竹制品计算和制定法律需要一定的时间,所以"等"也有等待的意思。

"等" is composed of "⺮" (zhú: bamboo) and "寺" (sì: temple). "⺮" stands for products of bamboo. In ancient times the Chinese used such products to count and engrave *Hanzi*. The temple in ancient times was a law enforcement agency. Therefore "等", made up of "⺮" and "寺", shows the counting and enacting laws that realize the aspiration of equality. It's an ideographic *zi*. To count or enact laws with products of bamboo, one needs a certain period of time, therefore "等" also means waiting.

(3) 开。"开"是"開"的简化字。"開"由"門"(门)和"开"组成,"开"由"一"和"廾"(gǒng)组成。"一"代表门闩,"廾"的古字像两手向上举物的样子。"開"(开)即用两手拉开门闩,以此表示"打开、开放"。指事字。

"开" is the simplified form of the *zi* for "開". "開" is composed of "門" (mén:door) and "开". "开" is composed of "一" and "廾" (gǒng). "一" stands for door bolt. The ancient form of the *zi* for "廾" is like holding something up with two hands. "開"(开) means to draw the door bolt with two hands, which stands for unfolding or opening up. It's a self-explanatory *zi*.

(4) 页。"页"的古字像坐着的人顶着一个大头,本义为"头"(tóu: head),借用为"页码"的"页"。

The ancient form of the *zi* for "页" (yè: head) is like a big headed person in a sitting position. Its original meaning is "head". Somehow it was later borrowed to take the meaning of "page".

(5) 顺。"顺"由"川"(chuān: river)和"页"(yè: head)组成。"川"的古字 ∭,两边像河岸,中间像流水,以此代表河流;"页"即"头"。"顺"示意水从头顶往下流,以此表示"顺当"。会意字。

"顺" is composed of "川" and "页". "川" (chuān: river) is a pictographic *zi*. The two sides for the ancient form of the *zi* for "川" are the river banks, while the middle stroke is surely flowing water. Together they stand for river. "页" (yè) means head. "顺" indicates the water comes down from the top of the head, which shows "smooth". It's an ideographic *zi*.

(6) 预。由"予"和"页"组成,"予"是音符,"页"即"头",表示"预"即事先用头脑思考。形声字。

"预" is composed of "予" (yǔ) and "页" (yè: head). "予" is the sound component and "页" is the meaning component. "预" means to think in advance, or use one's head. It's a picto-phonetic *zi*.

(7) 约。"约"由"纟"和"勺"组成。"约"又音"yāo","勺"为音符("勺"在"yuē"中不表音)。"纟"为义符。成束的丝可用于捆绑,以此表示"约"即"约束、束缚"。

"约" is composed of "纟" (sī: silk) and "勺" (sháo: spoon). "约" however has another pronunciation "yāo" in which "勺" is the sound component (but in "yuē" it does not indicate pronunciation.) and "纟" is the meaning component. Bundles of silk can be used to tie things up. This represents keeping with bounds, binding up.

(8) 男。"男"由"田"和"力"组成。田像方块田地的形状,"力"代表劳动。用在田里劳动的人代表男人。会意字。

男(nán: man, male) is formed of "田" (tián: farmland) and "力" (lì: strength; force). "田" is similar to a square-shaped farmland, and "力" stands for work. The person working in the field stands for man, the male. It's an ideographic *Hanzi*.

3. 字词用法例解 Explanation of the usages of *zi* and *zi*-groups

(1) 正在。"正在"的作用是放在表示动作的字词前面说明动作处于进行状态。"正在"也可以说成或写成"在"、"在……呢"、"正……呢"、"正在……呢"。例如:

"正在" put before an action *zi* or *zi*-group shows that an action is going on. "正在" can also appear as "在", "在……呢", "正……呢" and "正在……呢". For example:

① 马总正在会客。
② 他在喝茶。
③ 马太太正在打电话呢。
④ 王教授正吃午饭呢。
⑤ 林小姐在看书呢。

上面例子中的"呢"是语气助字,其作用是加强肯定的语气。

"呢", in the examples above works as a modal particle *zi*. It's function is to strengthen the affirmative tone.

否定动作正在进行的方法是在"在"前用"没"。例如:

The negative form of an action that's going on is to put "没" before "在". For example:

① 马总没在会客。
② 他没在喝茶。
③ 马太太没在打电话。
④ 王教授没在吃午饭。
⑤ 林小姐没在看书。

(2) "老……"和"小……"。"老、小"可以放在姓氏前作为称呼(例如"老马"、"小周")表示亲切。"老"一般用在中老年人的姓氏前面,"小"一般用在年轻人的姓氏前面。对长辈亲属(例如父亲、叔叔等)、老师和身份较高的人一般不这样称呼。

"老" and "小" preceding a surname (for instance, "老马" and "小周") can be used as a form of address and indicate closeness. Generally speaking, "老" comes before middle aged or old people's surname. "小" is normally used before young people's surname. However, people do not address their teachers, relatives (like father, uncle, etc), or other seniors in this way.

第二十七课　让您久等了
Lesson Twenty-seven
Sorry for Having Kept You Waiting So Long

一、部件 Components of *Hanzi*

1. 工部旁 the gōng left side
   工(项)（工 = 工）
2. 牛部边 the niú right side
   牛(件)（牛 niú cattle）
3. 贝部底 the bèi bottom
   贝(贺)（贝 bèi shell）

二、生字和生词 New *zi* and *zi*-groups

1. 让 (ràng) — allow; let; give way; give in; yield
   让开 — step aside; get out of the way
   让路 — make way for sb.or sth.
2. 散 (sàn) — break up; distribute; scatter
   散会 — (of a meeting) be over; break up
3. 刚 (gāng) — just; exactly; precisely
   刚刚 — 刚
4. 听 (tīng) — listen; hear
   听说 — be told; 听和说
5. 谈 (tán) — talk; speak; chat
   谈话 — conversation; talk; chat
   会谈 — talk; negotiation
6. 合 (hé) — close; come together; add up to
   合作 — cooperate; cooperation; work together; collaborate
   合同 (hétong) — contract

7.	项 (xiàng)	nape (of the neck); *a measure-zi*
	长项	strong point
8.	目 (mù)	eye; item
	项目	item; project
	合作项目	cooperation project; joint project
9.	于 (yú)	to; in; on; at
	等于	equal to; equivalent to
	关于	concerning; about; with regard to
10.	软 (ruǎn)	soft
11.	件 (jiàn)	letter; document; *a measure-zi*
	软件	software
12.	设 (shè)	set up; form
	设计	design; plan
13.	判	distinguish; judge
	谈判	negotiate; talk; negotiation
14.	董 (dǒng)	supervise; direct
15.	事 (shì)	matter; affair; thing; business
	董事	director; trustee
	办事	handle affairs; act; work
16.	长 (zhǎng)	chief; head
	董事长	chairman of the board
	司长	director of a department (in a ministry)
	会长	the president of an association or society
17.	签 (qiān)	sign
	签字	sign; affix one's signature
18.	订 (dìng)	conclude; draw up
	签订	conclude and sign
19.	协 (xié)	aid; assist
20.	议 (yì)	discuss; deliberate
	协议	agree on; agreement
	协议书	agreement
	签协议	sign an agreement
	会议	meeting; conference
	会议室	meeting room
21.	贺 (hè)	congratulate; celebrate

第二十七课　让您久等了

祝贺	congratulate; felicitate

※ ※ ※ ※ ※

久等	wait for a long time
说起	talk of
上周	last week
电子 (diànzǐ)	electron

三、补充生词　Supplementary zi-group

1. 散开　　　　　disperse
2. 散心　　　　　keep from worrying; relieve one's boredom
3. 打听　　　　　ask about; inquire about
4. 合计　　　　　amount to; total
5. 结合　　　　　combine; identify
6. 目前　　　　　present; current
7. 目的 (mùdì)　　purpose; goal
8. 题目　　　　　title; subject; topic; exercise problems; examination items
9. 国家项目　　　national project
10. 公司项目　　　company's project

四、唱读和口译　Read aloud and interpret

1. 刚
   刚来
   刚回来
   刚从上海回来
   刚到
   刚到这里
   刚走
   刚散会
   刚吃过午饭
   刚去过那里
2. 听说
   听说王教授身体不太好
   听说林小姐要回韩国
   听说林董事长要来中国

3. 关于
   关于合作的事
   关于合作项目
   关于软件设计
   关于生日晚会
4. 件
   软件
   一件事
   这件事

五、会话 Dialogue

让您久等了

周男：马总，三木先生来了，他在会客室等您。您散会了吗？
马总：三木先生来了？我们刚散会，我就来。
周男：三木先生，马总刚散会，他就来。
马总：对不起，三木先生，让你久等了，我们刚散会。
三木：我没有预约，路过这里，顺便来看看您。马太太好吗？
马总：她很好，天天上街买东西，也常常说起你和林小姐。听说你上周去上海了？
三木：是的，我昨天刚从上海回来，在那里谈了几个合作项目。
马总：是电子方面的吗？
三木：是关于软件设计的。
马总：这是你们的长项。谈判谈得怎么样？
三木：谈得非常好，林董事长下周来签订合作协议。
马总：太好了！这是大喜事，我祝贺你们！
三木：谢谢马总。

六、替换练习 Substitution drills

1. 三木先生来了，他在会客室等您。
   他说他想见您
   他说他要请您吃饭

2. 我路过这里,顺便来看看您。
   我来北京开会
   我到这里办事
   我路过你们公司

3. 我刚从上海回来,在那里谈了几个合作项目。
   在那里开了几天会
   在那里见到了几个老同学

4. 谈判谈得怎么样?
   说汉语说得
   学开车学得

1. 句法结构(2):基本句的组合生成 Sentence structure (2): formation of basic sentences

能够表示一个完整意思的独立的语言单位是句子。在书面汉语中,在句尾用句号(。)、问号(?)、叹号(!)等标点符号作为句子结束的标记。

A sentence is an independent language unit that expresses a complete idea. In written Chinese, a sentence is ended with a full stop, a question mark, an exclamation mark, etc.

根据结构规则,我们把汉语的句子分为基本句、复合句和复杂句三类。

According to the structure rules, we categorize Chinese sentences into three types: the basic sentence, the compound sentence and the complex sentence.

由一个主体和一个述体组合生成的句子是基本句。例如:

A sentence composed of a topic and a comment is called the basic sentence. For example:

① 马先生｜是中国人。
② 他｜有三本中文书。
③ 打的｜比较快。
④ 他们｜都喜欢喝绿茶。
⑤ 周男｜是从上海来的。

基本句与基本结构不是完全对应的,有些基本句的结构是复合结构。例如:
The basic sentence and the basic structure do not always correspond to each other, as some basic sentences are in compound structures. For example:

① 这｜是我妈给我的钱。
② 王师母｜身体非常好。
③ 下周｜他不在北京。
④ 听说｜你上周去上海了。
⑤ 我想｜请你辅导汉语。
⑥ 你知道｜北京饭店在哪儿吗?

在上面的例子中,主体/述体中带下划线的结构单位是基本结构,全句是复合结构。

Of the above examples, the underlined structures in the topics and / or comments are in basic structures, while the whole sentence in complex structures.

2. 字义例解和部件释义　Explanation of the meanings of *Hanzi* and *Hanzi* components

(1) 贝。"贝"的古字像张开的贝壳,以贝壳的形状代表"贝"。象形字。贝壳在古时可用于制造钱币,所以"贝"可以代表钱财。有"贝"作义符的汉字,其意思多半与"钱财、富有、尊贵"等有关。

The ancient form of the *Hanzi* for "贝"(bèi: shellfish)resembles an open shell. The shape of a shell stands for "贝". Shells in ancient times could be used for currency. Thus meanings of *Hanzi* with "贝" as a component are often related to wealth, richness, nobleness, etc.

(2) 目。"目"的古字像眼。有"目"作义符的汉字,其意思多半与眼睛和眼睛的动作等有关。

The ancient form of the *Hanzi* for "目"(mù: eye) is like the eye. The meanings of *Hanzi* with "目" as a meaning component are usually related to the eye or the action of the eyes.

(3) 牛。"牛"的古字像牛头的形状,以牛头的形状代表牛。象形字。

The ancient form of the *Hanzi* for "牛"(niú: cattle) resembles the shape of a cow's head, which, therefore, represents the cattle.

(4) 合。"合"的古字像器物和盖子相合的样子,以此代表"合起来"。指事字。

The ancient form of the *zi* for "合" resembles the shape of the closing of a utensil by the cover. This stands for "closing". It's a self-explanatory *zi*.

第二十七课　让您久等了

3. 字词用法例解 Explanation of the usages of *zi* and *zi*-groups

"的"字结构。"的"可以放在相关字词后面组成"的"字结构。"的"字结构的主要作用是对它后面的名字性成分加以修饰、限定,说明被修饰、被限定成分的所属、特点、类别等。例如:

The "的" structure. "的" could be put after a *zi* or *zi*-group to make the "的" structure. The main function of the "的" structure is to modify, restrict and explain the latter part's possession, characteristics, types, etc. For example:

① 这是他的书。
② 那是公司的项目。
③ 这个饭店的烤鸭很好。
④ 身体不好的人常常生病。
⑤ 这是我妈妈给我的钱。
⑥ 我的名字是"男女"的"男",不是"南方"的"南"

"的"字结构后面的被修饰、被限定的成分有时可以省去。例如:

The element that is modified or restricted by the "的" structure sometimes may be omitted. For example:

① 谢谢买单的(人)。
② 坐飞机来的(人)都吃过饭了。
③ 鲤鱼要清蒸的(鲤鱼)还是要红烧的(鲤鱼)?
④ 红烧的(鲤鱼)好。
⑤ 是电子方面的(项目)
⑥ 是关于软件设计的(项目)。

用"的"字结构代表从事某种职业或进行某种活动的人,含有轻蔑的意思。例如:

The "的" structure standing for a person engaged in a certain occupation or activity has an implication of contempt. For example:

① 他是开车的。(He is nothing but a car driver.)
② 她是开公司的。(She just runs a company.)

第二十八课　这是互利双赢的好项目

Lesson Twenty-eight　This is a Mutually Beneficial Win-win Project

一、部件　Components of *Hanzi*

1. 示部旁 the shì left side
   礻(视)（示 shì show; produce; instruct）(礻=示)
2. 衣部旁 the yī left side
   衤(补)（衣 yī clothing; clothes; dress）(衤=衣)
3. 弓部旁 the gōng left side
   弓(强)（弓 gōng bow; anything bow-shaped）
4. 巾部底 the jīn bottom
   巾(市)（巾 jīn a piece of cloth）
5. 正部底 the zhèng bottom
   疋(定)（疋=正）

二、生字和生词　New *zi* and *zi*-groups

1. 互 (hù)　　　　mutually
2. 利 (lì)　　　　benefits; interests
   有利　　　　advantageous; beneficial; favorable
   互利　　　　mutual benefit; of mutual benefit
3. 双 (shuāng)　even; double
   双方　　　　both sides; two parties
4. 赢 (yíng)　　win; gain profit
   赢利　　　　earn a profit
   双赢　　　　win-win
5. 希 (xī)　　　hope

第二十八课　这是互利双赢的好项目

6. 望（wàng）　　　　　　look or gaze into the distance; call on; pay a visit
　　看望　　　　　　　　call on; visit see
　　希望　　　　　　　　hope; wish; expect
7. 夫（fū）　　　　　　　husband; man; person engaged in manual labor
　　夫人（fūren）　　　　a lady of high rank; Madame; Mrs.;
　　　　　　　　　　　　the wife of a high official
8. 定（dìng）　　　　　　certainly; definitely; still; stable
　　一定　　　　　　　　definitely; inevitably; necessarily
9. 重（zhòng）　　　　　 be heavy; weighty; important
　　很重　　　　　　　　be very heavy
　　不重　　　　　　　　be not so heavy
10. 视（shì）　　　　　　look; view; look upon
　　电视　　　　　　　　television
　　电视机　　　　　　　television set
　　重视　　　　　　　　attach importance to; think highly of; lay stress on
11. 算（suàn）　　　　　 calculate; estimate
　　计算　　　　　　　　count; calculate
　　计算机　　　　　　　computer
12. 市（shì）　　　　　　market; municipality
　　市场　　　　　　　　marketplace; market
　　市面　　　　　　　　market
　　北京市　　　　　　　Beijing municipality
　　市长　　　　　　　　mayor
13. 平（píng）　　　　　 flat; level; smooth; make it a level
　　水平　　　　　　　　standard; level
　　设计水平　　　　　　level of design
　　汉语水平　　　　　　Chinese language proficiency
14. 发（fā）　　　　　　 give out; distribute; produce; develop; expand
　　发生　　　　　　　　happen; occur; arise; take place
　　开发　　　　　　　　develop; exploit
15. 力（lì）　　　　　　 force; strength; power; ability
　　能力　　　　　　　　ability; capability; capacity
　　有力　　　　　　　　strong; powerful; vigorous
16. 强（qiáng）　　　　　be strong; be powerful; mighty
　　很强　　　　　　　　be very powerful
　　不强　　　　　　　　be not so strong

17.	取 (qǔ)	get; draw; select
18.	补 (bǔ)	repair; mend
19.	短 (duǎn)	be short; brief
	很短	be very short
	不短	be not short
	取长补短	learn from each other's strong points to offset one's own weaknesses
20.	成 (chéng)	accomplish; succeed
	成为	become; urn into
	建成	succeed in building
	谈成	succeed in negotiating
	做成	accomplish; attain; achieve
21.	功 (gōng)	achievement; merit; effect; success
	成功	success; successful
	用功	work hard

三、补充生词 Supplementary zi-group

1.	工夫 (gōngfu)	time; skill
2.	安定	stable; quiet; settled
3.	重要	important; significant; essential; major
4.	重点	key point; emphasis; focus
5.	市场开发	market development
6.	开发市场	develop the market
7.	发奖	award prizes; present prizes
8.	发现	find; discover; detect; become aware of; discovery
9.	和平	peaceful; peace
10.	平等	equal; equality
11.	强大	big and strong; powerful
12.	成双	form a pair
13.	成语	idiom
14.	成就	achievement; accomplishment
15.	算账	do or work out accounts
16.	打算 (dǎsuan)	intend; plan; think of; consideration

第二十八课　这是互利双赢的好项目

四、唱读和口译　Read aloud and interpret

1. 希望
   希望早日见到你
   希望你们合作成功
   希望你常常来北京
   希望大家都喜欢
   有希望
   有成功的希望
   没希望
   没成功的希望
2. 一定
   一定来
   一定很高兴
   一定能成功
   一定有希望
   不一定
   不一定能来
   不一定能成功
   不一定有希望
3. 重视
   很重视
   不重视
   很重视这件事
   很重视这个项目
   很重视上海的合作项目

五、会话　Dialogue

这是个互利双赢的好项目

三木：林董事长要我替他向您问好。
马总：谢谢！我和林董事长是老朋友了。希望他这次也来北京。
三木：他会来的,他说他要来看望您。
马总：董事长夫人也来吗？
三木：她也来,她要来看她女儿。
马总：太好了！我太太知道了,一定很高兴。
三木：林董事长非常重视上海的合作项目。

马总：计算机软件市场很大。

三木：这家上海公司的软件设计水平很
　　　高，可是市场开发能力不强。

马总：你们的市场开发能力很强，双方
　　　合作可以取长补短。

三木：林董事长说，这是个互利双赢的
　　　好项目。

马总：林董事长很有远见。希望你们合作成功。

三木：我想一定能成功。

六、替换练习　Substitution drills

1. 这是<u>互利双赢</u>的好项目。
   能很快赢利
   市场很大
   大家都喜欢

2. 林董事长要我<u>替他向您问好</u>。
   替他来看望您
   替他请您吃饭
   替他签字

3. 他说<u>他要来看望您</u>。
   他一定来
   他很想见到您
   这是一件大好事
   这是个互利双赢的好项目
   这项合作一定能成功

4. 我想<u>一定能成功</u>。
   这是个互利双赢的好项目
   这是一件大好事
   没有人不喜欢这件事

第二十八课　这是互利双赢的好项目

1. 句法结构（3）：复合句的组合生成 Sentence structure (3): formation of compound sentences

由两个和两个以上语义相关并用逗号隔开的基本句组合生成的句子是复合句。例如：

The compound sentence is composed of two or more basic sentences, which are semantically related and spaced with a comma. For example:

① 马先生｜不在家,‖他｜还没有回来呢。
② 我妈妈｜要给你打电话,‖她｜想请你吃饭。
③ 林小姐｜也喜欢吃烤鸭,‖她｜还喜欢吃鱼。
④ 多数南方人｜喜欢吃米饭,‖多数北方人｜喜欢吃面食。
⑤ 他｜在办公室,‖你｜可以给他办公室打电话。
⑥ 您｜打他的手机吧,‖他的手机号码｜是13301010788。
⑦ 你｜是个大忙人,‖我｜不敢麻烦你。
⑧ 白天｜工作很忙,‖晚上｜还要学习。
⑨ 中午｜不能喝酒,‖下午｜还要工作。
⑩ 三木｜是日本人,‖林正美｜是韩国人,‖马先生和马太太｜都是中国人。

以上例句中双竖线前后的都是基本句。复合句中的基本句也叫分句。

In each of the sentences above the two parts on either side of the parallel are basic sentences or clauses.

由一个基本句和与该基本句语义相关的其他成分组合生成、基本句与其他成分之间用逗号隔开的句子也是复合句。例如：

Compound sentences may also be composed of one basic sentence and other elements semantically related, which are spaced with a comma. For example：

① 在北京饭店,‖你｜知道北京饭店在哪儿吗？
② 不过没关系‖我｜可以问人。
③ 要是坐公共汽车,‖多长时间｜能到？
④ 再来一瓶红酒吧,‖我妈和林小姐｜都能喝红酒。

⑤ 不用客气。‖ 星期六 ｜ 见。
⑥ 有红茶,也有绿茶,‖ 您 ｜ 喝红茶还是喝绿茶?
⑦ 我 ｜ 没去过, ‖ 好像在长安街。
⑧ 她 ｜ 很好, ‖ 天天上街买东西,也常常说起你和林小姐。
⑨ 我 ｜ 没预约, ‖ 路过这里,顺便来看看您。
⑩ 您 ｜ 汉语 ｜ 说得真好, ‖ 是在哪儿学的?

2. 字义例解和部件释义　Explanation of the meanings of *Hanzi* and *Hanzi* components

(1) 巾。"巾"的古字巾像下垂的布。象形字。有"巾"作义符的汉字,其意思多半与纺织品等有关。

The ancient form of the *Hanzi* for "巾" (jīn: kerchief, scarf, etc.) is like a piece of drooping cloth. It's a pictographic *zi*. The meanings of *Hanzi* with "巾" as a meaning component are often related to textiles.

(2) 市。"市"由"亠"和"巾"(jīn)组成。"亠"代表建筑,"巾"代表商品(古代的商品主要是纺织品),以有建筑和商品的地方代表市场、城市。会意字。

"市" is composed of "亠" and "巾" (jīn), with "亠" standing for building and "巾" merchandise(In ancient times, products mainly referred to textile products). A place with building and merchandise represent market, city. It's an ideographic *zi*.

(3) 礻。"礻"是"示"作部旁时的变体。"示"的古字示像想象中的地神(dìshén: local god of the land)的形状,在现代汉字中只作部旁和义符。有"礻"作义符的汉字,其意思多半与神、祸、福、祝贺以及某些精神活动等有关。

"礻" (shì: divinity) is the variant of "示" used as a left component. In ancient times, the shape of "示" looked like a local god of the land. In modern Chinese it's only used as a left meaning component. *Hanzi* with this component usually signifies something about god, disaster, good fortune, congratulation, mental activities, etc.

(4) 衤。"衤"是"衣"作部旁时的变体,用作义符。"衣"的古字衣像上衣的形状,以上衣的形状代表衣服。有"衤"(衣)作义符的汉字,其意思多半与服装等有关。

"衤" (yī: clothes) is the variant of "衣" when used as a left meaning component. The ancient form of the *zi* for "衣" is like the shape of an upper garment which represents clothes. The meanings of *Hanzi* with the component "衤" are often related to clothes, etc.

(5) 补。"补"由"衤"和"卜"(bǔ)组成,"衤"是义符,"卜"是音符。"补"的本义是缝补衣服,引申为"补充"。形声字。

第二十八课　这是互利双赢的好项目

"补" is composed of "衤" (yī: clothes) and "卜" (bǔ), with "衤" being the meaning component and "卜" the sound component. The original meaning of "补" is to mend clothes. Later it was extended to "supplement". It's a picto-phonetic *zi*.

(6) 利。"利"由"禾"和"刂"组成，"禾"代表庄稼。"利"即用刀收割庄稼，以此代表收获、有利、顺利等。会意字。

"利" is composed of "禾" (hé: standing grain) and "刂" (dāo: knife). "禾" stands for agricultural plant. "利" means to reap crops. This stands for harvest, beneficial, smooth, etc. It's an ideographic *zi*.

(7) 力。"力"的古字 像一种农具，使用这种农具必须用力。指事字。有"力"作义符的汉字，其意思多与用力有关。

The ancient form of the *Hanzi* for "力" (lì: force) is like a sort of farming tool. People have to exert strength to use the tool. It's an indicative *zi*. The meanings of *Hanzi* with the meaning component "力" are often related to force or strength.

(8) 廾。"廾"是古"拱"字， 像两手相对向上捧物。在现代汉字中只作义符。有"廾"作义符的汉字多半是动字。

"廾" (gǒng) is the ancient form of the *Hanzi* for "拱" (gǒng) that resembles holding up something with two hands facing each other. In modern *Hanzi* "廾" is only used as a meaning component. Most of the *Hanzi* with "廾" as a meaning component are action-*zi*.

(9) 算。"算"的古字上面像竹，中间像算盘珠，下面像手的动作，表示用手拨算盘珠，是计算的意思。算盘是中国的一种计算工具。指事字。

The top of the ancient *Hanzi* for "算" (suàn: calculate) is like bamboo, the middle component is like an abacus chu, and the bottom part is like the action of hand. The *Hanzi* for "算" as a whole therefore signifies the moving of an abacus with a hand. Abacus is a kind of calculating apparatus. It's a self-explanatory *zi*.

(10) 定。"定"由"宀"和"疋"(正)组成。"宀"代表房屋，"疋"(正)代表垂直。以房屋垂直表示固定。会意字。

"定" is composed of "宀" and "疋". "宀" stands for a house while "疋" indicates uprightness. The uprightness of a house indicates fixity. It's an ideographic *zi*.

3. 字词用法例解　Explanation of the usages of *zi* and *zi*-groups

(1) 夫人。"夫人"一般用于称呼或称谓身份地位较高者的妻子。

"夫人" is often used to address the wife of a high ranking person.

(2) 他会来的。这里的"会"要重读。"他会来的"是"他是会来的"的意思，强调说明他一定来。

"他会来的" means "他是会来的", among which "会" is accentuated and emphasizes the certainty of his coming.

第二十九课　贵客到了
Lesson Twenty-nine　The Distinguished Guest is Arriving

一、部件　Components of *Hanzi*

1. 彡部旁 the shān left side
   彡(须)（彡 shān beard）
2. 耳部旁 the ěr left side
   耳(职)（耳 ěr ear）
3. 土部旁 the tǔ left side
   ㇀(地)（土 tǔ soil）（㇀=土）

二、生字和生词　New *zi* and *zi*-groups

1. 乱 (luàn) — in disorder
2. 沙 (shā) — sand
   沙发 (shāfā) — sofa
3. 爸 (bà) — pa; dad
   爸爸 (bàba) — 爸
4. 消 (xiāo) — disappear
   消气 — cool down; be mollified
5. 息 (xī) — cease; stop
   消息 (xiāoxi) — information
6. 参 (cān) — participate
7. 加 (jiā) — add; plus; put in
   参加 — join; take part in
8. 须 (xū) — beard; must; have to
   必须 — must; have to
9. 由 (yóu) — by sb; by means of
   由……做东 — ...play the host

10. 感 (gǎn) — feel; sense; be aware
    感谢 — thank; be thankful; be grateful
11. 情 (qíng) — feeling; situation
    热情 — warm; warmth
    友情 — friendly sentiments
    心情 — frame of mind; mood
12. 地 (de) — land; *a structural particle used after an adverbial*
    热情地 (de) — warmly
13. 照 (zhào) — shine; light up
    关照 — look after; take care of
14. 顾 (gù) — turn round and look at; take into consideration
    照顾 — look after; care for
15. 满 (mǎn) — full; complete; completely
    期满 — expired; come to an end
16. 后 (hòu) — behind; back; after; afterwards
    后门 — back door (or gate)
    后年 — the year after next
    后天 — the day after tomorrow
    以后 — afterwards; later on
    最后 — lastly; finally
17. 式 (shì) — style; type; fashion
    样式 — pattern; style; type; fashion
    正式 — formal
    非正式 — 不是正式的
18. 职 (zhí) — duty; job; position
    职工 — workers and staff members
    就职 — accession; take up an appointment; assume office
19. 担 (dān) — carry on a shoulder pole; take on; undertake
    担心 — worry; feel anxious; fear
20. 辈 (bèi) — generation
    一辈子 — all one's life; life time
21. 句 (jù) — sentence
    句子 — 句
    一句话 — (have) a word
22. 死 (sǐ) — die; be dead; to the death
    高兴死了 — be extremely happy

23.	玩 (wán)	play; have fun
	玩儿	玩
24.	笑 (xiào)	smile; laugh
	玩笑	joke
	开玩笑	crack a joke; make fun of

※ ※ ※ ※ ※

	贵客	honoured guest
	由于	owing to; due to; as a result of
	一年多	one year and more
	以来	since
	总是	always; at all time
	关心	be concerned with; care for
	一起	together
	实习期	the period of practice
	哪能	how can; how could

三、补充生词 Supplementary zi-group

1.	须要	须
2.	须知	one should know that; points for attention
3.	加强	strengthen; intensify; enhance; reinforce
4.	感到	feel; sense
5.	感想	impressions; reflections; thought
6.	事情	事
7.	满月	full moon; one full month after birth
8.	后方	behind; at the back
9.	后来	afterwards; later
10.	后人	later generations
11.	职业	occupation; profession; vocation
12.	职员	clerk; office worker; staff member
13.	公式	formula
14.	前辈	the older generation; senior (person); elder
15.	晚辈	the younger generation
16.	笑话	joke; jest

四、唱读和口译 Read aloud and interpret

1. 消息
   有什么消息
   没有消息
   好消息
   有个好消息
   刚听到的消息
   晚来的消息
   很关心马建的消息

2. 参加
   参加工作
   参加谈判
   参加生日晚会

3. 必须
   必须参加
   必须成功
   必须去看王教授
   必须由我做东

4. 一起,和……一起
   他们在一起
   我们一起去吧
   他们一起在北京饭店吃饭
   三木和林正美一起去给王教授祝寿了
   林正美要和她父母一起回国

5. 正式
   正式职工
   正式职业
   正式工作

6. 就
   早就认识了
   就来
   一会儿就来
   十分钟就到
   车站就在那儿
   以后就是正式职工了
   那就太好了

第二十九课 贵客到了

就叫我小周吧
就在沙发上坐吧

7. 担心
很担心
非常担心
担心您的身体
担心他的健康
担心她不回来

8. 哪能
哪能让您请我？
哪能让您不高兴？
我哪能走在您前面？
王教授岁数大了，哪能让他坐公共汽车？

9. 死
死了
没死
不能死
不会死
高兴死了（非常高兴）
担心死了（非常担心）
累死了（非常累）

10. 地
热情地关心
热情地欢迎
高兴地说

五、会话 Dialogue

贵客到了

林小姐：马太太好！

马太太：贵客到了，欢迎！我家里很乱，你就在这里的沙发上坐吧。

林小姐：马太太，我爸爸和妈妈下周来北京。

马太太：我先生回来说了，这是个好消息。听说你父母要来北京，我们都非常高兴。

林小姐：他们要请您和马先生吃饭，请马建和马阳也参加。

马太太：在北京我们是主人，必须由我们做东。

林小姐：马太太不必客气，我爸爸、妈妈这次来北京，是专门来感谢您和马先生的。这一年多以来，你们总是热情地关心我，给了我很多照顾。

马太太：这都是应该的。听说你要和你父母一起回国？

林小姐：是的，我的实习期满了。不过还要再来，以后就是正式职工了。

马太太：那就太好了！马建听说你要回国，还担心你不回来呢。

林小姐：哪能不回来？我一辈子都要在中国工作。

马太太：真的吗？马建听到你这句话，一定要高兴死了！

林小姐：马太太真会开玩笑！

六、替换练习 Substitution drills

1. <u>听说你父母要来北京</u>，我们都非常高兴。
   听说你们的合作很成功
   听到这个好消息
   看到您身体这样好
   您能参加这个会
   您能和我们一起工作

2. <u>马建听到你这句话</u>，一定要高兴死了！
   大家听到这个好消息
   他知道他能成为北大的学生

3. 不过还要再来，以后就<u>是正式职工了</u>。
   在这里工作了
   在这里长住了
   是这里的主人了
   不会离开你了

4. <u>马太太</u>真会开玩笑！
   大家
   你们
   你

第二十九课 贵客到了

汉语知识
Chinese Language ABC

1. 句法结构(4)：复杂句的组合生成 Sentence structure (4): combination of complex sentences

由两个或两个以上的分句组成，分句与分句之间语义关系比较复杂的句子是复杂句。我们学过的复杂句不多，仅举数例如下：

Complex sentences are composed of two or more clauses and the semantic relations between the clauses are relatively complicated. We haven't learned much complex sentences, a few examples are as follows:

① 对不起，三木先生，让你久等了，我们刚散会。
② 再要一碗米饭，我太太是南方人，她喜欢吃米饭。
③ 我以前不喜欢吃面食，现在也喜欢了，面条、包子、饺子我都爱吃。
④ 我叫周男，是总经理办公室的秘书，您就叫我小周吧。
⑤ 对，我是上海人，不过我的名字是"男女"的"男"，不是"南方"的"南"。
⑥ 马太太不必客气，我爸爸、妈妈这次来北京，是专门来感谢您和马先生的。

2. 字义例解和部件释义 Explanation of the meanings of *Hanzi* and *Hanzi* components

(1) 彡(shān)。"彡"的古字像胡须。本义为毛发、花纹，在现代汉字中只作义符。有"彡"作义符的汉字，其意思多与毛发、外形等有关。

"彡" (shān). The ancient form of the *Hanzi* for "彡" is like a man's beard. Its original meaning is hair, decorative patterns. In modern *Hanzi*, it's just used as a meaning component. Meanings of *Hanzi* with this "彡" component are usually related to hair, appearance, etc.

(2) 耳。"耳"的古字像耳朵的形状，以耳朵的形状代表"耳"。象形字。

The ancient form of the *zi* for "耳" (ér: ear) looks like the shape of an ear. It's a pictographic *zi*.

(3) 由。"由"为"田"字中的竖(丨)出头，出头部分表示从此进田。意为"从"。指事字。

"由" (yóu: start from) is similar to "田" (tián: field) with the vertical stroke in the middle crossing the horizontal stroke on the top. The extended stroke indicates an entrance to the field. Thus it means "from". It's an indicative *zi*.

(4) 加。"加"由"力"和"口"组成,"口"在这里代表"人","加"就是"把人的力量合起来"。会意字。

"加" is composed of "力" (lì: force) and "口". "口" stands for a person. "加" means to put people's strength together. It's an ideographic *zi*.

(5) 土。"土"的古字像地上的小土块。象形字。作部旁时写做"扌"。

The ancient form of the *Hanzi* for "土" (earth, soil) is like a small lump of soil. It's a pictographic *zi*. When used as a left component, it's written as "扌".

3. 字词用法例解 Explanation of the usages of *zi* and *zi*-groups

是的。"是的"用于对对方的陈述表示肯定,也可以说"是"。

"是的" or "是" is used to express approval to the other party's statement.

第三十课　复习（六）
Lesson Thirty　Review（6）

一、说出下列部件的名称 Read aloud the following components

1. 一(六)
2. 丶(总)
3. ナ(有)
4. 勹(包)
5. 小(尝)
6. 宀(安)
7. 艹(茶)
8. 耂(老)
9. 手(看)
10. 覀(要)
11. 竹(等)
12. 厶(么)
13. 力(方)
14. 灬(蒸)
15. 疋(定)
16. 止(走)

17. 木(条)
18. 亻(体)
19. 彳(街)
20. 讠(说)
21. 冫(凉)
22. 氵(海)
23. 彡(须)
24. 饣(饮)
25. 工(项)
26. 女(姐)
27. 纟(红)
28. 忄(情)
29. 扌(打)
30. 木(林)
31. 火(烤)
32. 车(辅)

33. 王(现)
34. 钅(钟)
35. 礻(祝)
36. 衤(补)
37. 矢(知)
38. 立(站)
39. 足(路)
40. 刂(到)
41. 攵(做)
42. 戋(钱)
43. 口(国)
44. 冂(用)
45. 辶(远)
46. 丰(用)
47. 文(这)

二、朗读下列各组汉字，说出每组汉字中相同部件的名称 Read aloud the following *Hanzi* and tell the common name of components of *Hanzi* in each group

1. 安　定　家　客　实　室　宜　字
2. 分　公　关　美
3. 贵　贺　员
4. 菜　茶　董　英　蒸
5. 辅　软　斩
6. 到　刚　判

7. 烦　烤　烧
8. 点　热　照　蒸
9. 号　员　只
   吧　吃　喝　叫　吗　哪　呢　听
   和　加　知
   合　名　喜
   回　问　向　句　可
   豆　高　京　总
10. 加　功　男
11. 机　林　条
12. 好　姐　妈　她　姓
    安　要
13. 敢　教　散　数　做
14. 便　候　件　健　你　什　体　位　像　优　作　做
15. 是　星　早　最
    明　时　晚　昨　阳
    替
    间
16. 给　红　结　经　绿　绍　约
17. 饱　饭　饺　饮
18. 打　担　接　授　找　折
19. 海　汉　酒　没　汽　消
20. 感　惠　您　息　想　怎　总
21. 快　利　忙　情
22. 该　话　计　请　让　认　设　谁　识　说　谈　谢　议　语
23. 烦　顾　顺　项　须　预
24. 道　过　还　近　迎　这

三、朗读下列汉字,并说出每个汉字的义符 Read aloud the following *Hanzi* and tell the names of the meaning components

病　餐　凉　钱　算　视　祝　账

四、朗读下列汉字,并说出每个汉字的音符 Read aloud the following *Hanzi* and tell the names of the sound components

功　健　理　鲤　码　清　钟　机　吗
妈　近　请　情　望　远　账　职　问

五、朗读下列常用语句 Read aloud the following frequently used sentences

1. 贵客到了,欢迎!
2. 您请里面坐。
3. 我家里很乱,你就在沙发上坐吧。
4. 您请喝水。
5. 对不起,让你久等了。
6. 这是大喜事,我祝贺你们!
7. 林董事长要我替他向您问好。
8. 我太太知道了,一定很高兴。
9. 马建听到你这句话,一定要高兴死了!
10. 马太太真会开玩笑!

六、朗读下面的句子,并说出每个句子的主体 Read aloud the following sentences and find out the topic of each sentence

1. 我是王先生的学生。
2. 马飞先生是中国人吗?
3. 马飞先生是不是有两个儿子?
4. 马太太不是北京人,她是上海人。
5. 昨天是马建的生日。
6. 他的手机号码是13301010788。
7. 这是我妈给我的钱,我妈的钱比我多。
8. 我有三本书。
9. 林董事长很有远见。
10. 姐到了,我们点菜。
15. 我想一定能成功。
16. 打的比较快,十分钟就到。
17. 见到你们我很高兴
18. 下次请你们吃西餐。
19. 下回我做东。
20. 中午不能喝酒,下午还要工作。

七、朗读下面的句子,并说出每个句子的述体 Read aloud the following sentences and find out the comment of each sentence

1. 我是去看马建的。
2. 他们身体很好。
3. 你的汉语很好。
4. 红烧的好。
5. 计算机软件市场很大。
6. 总经理在吗?
7. 马先生不在家。
8. 他在会客室等您。
9. 你知道北京饭店在哪儿吗?
10. 北京饭店在天安门广场东面。
11. 我在公司实习。
12. 他在北京大学学习。
13. 我们在一家韩国公司工作。
14. 我在这儿学过四年。
15. 林董事长要我替他向您问好。
16. 林董事长很重视上海的合作项目。
17. 你喝茶还是喝咖啡?
18. 您喝红茶还是喝绿茶?
19. 鲤鱼要清蒸的还是要红烧的?
20. 林小姐吃得很少。
21. 我吃得太多了。
22. 我好久没吃面条了。

八、说话练习 Oral practice

说说三木会见马飞和林小姐会见马太太的情况(qíngkuàng: situation)。

1. 三木和马飞是在哪里见面的?
2. 三木到那里的时候,马飞在做什么?是谁接待(jiēdài: receive)他的?
3. 说说周男的情况。
4. 三木给马飞提供(tígòng: provide)了什么消息?
5. 马飞认为他们的合作项目怎么样?为什么说这是个互利双赢的好项目?

第三十课 复习(六)

6. 林小姐的父亲是什么人？他为什么要来上海？什么要来北京？
7. 马飞认识林小姐的父亲吗？你怎么知道？.
8. 林正美去马建家了吗？她是去做什么的？
9. 马太太为什么说"马建听到你这句话，一定要高兴死了"？
10. 林小姐为什么说"马太太真会开玩笑"？

九、说快板儿 Read and recite a clapper talk

姓氏歌
A rhyme of surnames

上有口,下有口,
上口下口双口吕；
左有木,右有木,
左木右木双木林。

上有木,下有子。
上木下子木子李。
木子李,十八子
两种说法都有理。

左有弓,右有长(zhǎng),
左弓右长弓长张。
弓长(zhǎng)张,弓长(cháng)张
两个说法都是张。

上有立,下有早,
上立下早立早章。
立早章,弓长张
两个姓,不一样。

左有阝(阜：fù),右有东,
左阝右东他姓陈。
左有关,右有阝(邑：yì),
左关右阝她姓郑。
阝(fù)是山,阝(yì)是城,
左山右城要区分。

107

汉语速成·基础篇(下册)

生字和生词

1. 姓氏 (xìngshì)   姓
2. 吕 (Lǚ)   *a surname*
3. 李 (Lǐ)   *a surname*
4. 张 (Zhāng)   *a surname*
5. 章 (Zhāng)   *a surname*
6. 陈 (Chén)   *a surname*
7. 郑 (Zhèng)   *a surname*
8. 山 (shān)   hill; mountain
9. 城 (chéng)   city
10. 区分 (qūfēn)   distinguish

附录1 汉语音节的语音结构和书写方法
Appendix 1 Phonetic structures and spelling rules of Chinese syllables

汉语音节的语音结构和书写方法 Phonetic structures and spelling rules of Chinese syllables

1. 汉语音节的语音结构 The phonetic structure of Chinese syllables

汉语的音节有言语音节和语言音节之分。

言语音节是音义单位,也是口头汉语的基本单位。例如:

Chinese syllables can be divided into speech syllables and language syllables. Speech syllables are both phonetic and semantic units as well as the basic units in oral Chinese. For example:

① wǒmen

② xuéxí

③ Hànyǔ

④ wǒmen xuéxí Hànyǔ.

上面是用汉语拼音书写的言语音节和大于言语音节的言语单位。例①~③是词,例④是句子,音节之间都用空格隔开。这些音节都有固定的音和义,所以是音义单位;词和句子都是由音节组合生成的,可见这些音节也是口头汉语的基本单位。

The above speech syllables spelled with *Hanyu Pinyin* are speech units larger than speech syllables. Examples ①~③ are *zi*-groups, while ④ is a sentence, all with a blank spaced between syllables. All these syllables are phonetically and semantically fixed, so they are phonetic and semantic units. Both *zi*-groups and sentences are formed of syllables, therefore these syllables are basic units in oral Chinese as well.

语言音节是单纯的语音单位。汉语音节的语音结构是指语音单位的结构。

Language syllables are purely phonetic units. The phonetic structures of Chinese syllables are those of phonetic units.

从语音结构的角度说,一个音节一般由一个声母、一个韵母和一个声调三部分组成,声母、韵母和声调就是汉语音节语音结构的生成元素。音节开头的部分是声母,结尾的部分是

韵母,每一个音节都有一个固定的声调,代表音节发音的高低升降。例如:

In Chinese normally a syllable is composed of an initial, a final and a tone. Initials, finals and tones are combinative elements of phonetic structures of Chinese syllables. The initial comes at the beginning of a syllable and the final the rest of it. Each syllable and its corresponding *Hanzi* have a certain tone, standing for the modulation in pronunciation. For example:

① xué ← xue ← x·üe

② hàn ← han ← h·an

上面例①中的 x 是声母,ue 是韵母,é 上面的符号代表声调;例②中的 h 是声母,an 是韵母,à 上面的符号代表声调。

In ① above "x" is the initial, "üe" the final and the sign on the top of "e" the tone. In ②, "h" is the initial, "an" the final, and the sign on the top of "a" the tone.

有些音节没有声母,没有声母的音节叫零声母音节;例如:

Some syllables have no initials and are called zero initial syllables. For example:

ài(爱)   ān(安)   èr(二)

还有少量音节没有韵母,没有韵母的音节叫零韵母音节。例如:

And a few syllables have no finals and are called zero final syllables. For example:

m(呣)   ng(嗯)

每一个音节都是一个整体,发音时要一气呵成,声母和韵母之间没有任何停顿,声调更不能独立存在。但是了解音节的语音结构对学好音节的发音有一定的帮助。一个音节的发音是否正确,可以从声母、韵母和声调这三个方面加以鉴别;学习过程中发生的发音偏误就表现在这三个方面,纠正发音偏误也要从这三个方面纠正。

Every syllable is an integral whole and that is the way to pronounce it, with no pause between the initial and the final. It is helpful to the learning of pronouncing the syllables, if one has some knowledge of the phonetic structure of a syllable. If one can pronounce the initial, the final and tone of a syllable properly, we say he or she has pronounced the syllable correctly. When we are aware that an error in pronunciation (that of initial, final or tone) has occurred, we can correct them accordingly.

1.1 汉语音节的声母。汉语音节的声母全部由辅音充任。辅音就是气流在发音器官里受到阻碍而形成的一类音素。现代汉语普通话的全部音节包括下列 21 个声母:

Initials of Chinese syllables. All initials are consonants. The consonant is a type of sound that is produced by stopping the air in the articulation organs before releasing it out. In modern Chinese the following 21 initials can be identified in all the syllables:

b   p   m   f
d   t   n   l
g   k   h
j   q   x
zh   ch   sh   r
z   c   s

附录1 汉语音节的语音结构和书写方法

1.2 汉语音节的韵母。汉语音节的韵母由单元音、复元音和元音加鼻辅音充任。元音就是气流在口腔里受不到阻碍而形成的一类音素。现代汉语普通话共有36个韵母,其中单元音韵母6个,复元音韵母13个,元音加鼻辅音韵母16个,儿化韵韵母1个。

Finals of Chinese syllables. In Chinese simple vowels, compound vowels and nasal vowels can serve as finals. The vowel is a type of sound that is produced with the air in the mouth coming out freely. In modern Chinese there are altogether 36 vowels, including 6 simple finals, 13 compound finals, 16 nasal finals and 1 retroflex final.

(1) 单元音韵母 **The simple finals are**:

　　a　o　e　i　u　ü

(2) 复元音韵母 **The compound finals are:**

　　ai　ei　ao　ou　ia　ie　ua　uo　üe
　　iao　iou　uai　uei

(3) 元音加鼻辅音韵母 **The nasal finals are:**

　　an　en　ian　in　uan　uen　üan　ün
　　ang　eng　ong　iang　ing　iong　uang　ueng

(4) 儿化韵韵母 **The retroflexed final is:**

　　er

1.3 汉语音节的声调　The tones of Chinese Syllables

声调是指音节发音的高低升降,用来区别不同的字义。

Tones refer to the modulation of sound pitch when pronouncing a Chinese syllable. The function of the tone is to differentiate meanings.

1.3.1 调型。按高低升降的程度分类,汉语的声调分为第一声、第二声、第三声、第四声、轻声和半三声六种调型。

Types of the tone: Six types of tones are specified according to the changes of pitch: the first tone, the second tone, the third tone, the fourth tone, the neutral tone and the half-third tone.

(1) 第一声。第一声是高平调,例如:

　　The first tone is a high and level tone. For example:

　　一　三　七　八　他

(2) 第二声。第二声是升调,例如:

　　The second tone is a rising tone. For example:

　　十　人　来　王　门

(3) 第三声。第三声是降升调,例如:

　　The third tone is a falling-rising tone. For example:

　　五　你　几　姐　语

(4) 第四声。第四声是降调,例如:

　　The fourth tone is a falling tone. For example:

　　二　四　六　去　木

(5) 轻声。轻声是轻而短的调型,它的高低程度随着它前面一个音节声调的高低程度而有所不同。也就是说,轻声是随着它前面一个音节声调的高低程度发得又轻又短的声调。例如:

The neutral tone is a light and short tone whose pitch varies with that of the previous syllable. For example:

(他)们　(来)了　(你)呢　(贵)吗

轻声音节数量不多,主要的有:

The number of neutral tone syllables is not large. Mainly they are:

a　ba　bo　da　de　e　la　li　le　ma　me　men　na　ne　qu　wa　ya　zhe　zi

(6) 半三声。半三声是第三声的变调。第三声与它后面的第一声、第二声、第四声和轻声音节组合时,调型变为接近低平,只是略有降升。例如:

The half-third tone is a variant of the third tone. When it is followed by a first, second, fourth or neutral tone syllable, a third tone syllable changes to a low level tone with but a slight rising. For example:

第三声＋第一声　The third tone＋the first tone

马飞　你说　两天　五星

第三声＋第二声　The third tone＋the second tone

九十　你来　女人　美国

第三声＋第四声　The third tone＋the fourth tone

我会　也去　怎样　很贵

第三声＋轻声　The third tone＋the neutral tone

我的　你呢　有了　好吗

1.3.2 调型变化。汉语音节的调型变化叫变调。变调不是上述六种调型之外的调型,而是指有些音节在与其他音节组合时的调型变化。除了上述半三声之外,还有轻声变调、第二声变调和个别变调。

Changes of tone. The changes of tone types of Chinese syllables are called modified tones, which are not a tone type beside the six types mentioned above. It refers to the tone-changes when a syllable is followed by other syllables. Apart from the half-third tone, there are changes of the four tones to the neutral tone, change of the third tone to the second tone and tone changes of individual *Hanzi*.

(1) 轻声变调。有些音节本来不是轻声,但用在某些音节的后面要改发轻声。例如:

Changes of the four tones to the neutral tone. Some syllables themselves are not in the neutral tone, but they are pronounced in the neutral tone when they are preceded by some other syllables or *Hanzi*.

子→本子　儿→女儿　里→这里

(2) 第二声变调。两个第三声音节组合时,前面的第三声音节要改发第二声。例如:

Change of the third tone to the second tone. When two third tones syllables come in succession, the first one changes to the second tone.

两本　子女　口语　很好　请你

(3) 个别变调:个别变调主要有"不"和"一"的变调。

附录 1　汉语音节的语音结构和书写方法

Tone changes of individual *Hanzi*. This mainly refers to the tone changes of "不" and "一".

"不"的变调。"不"的原调是第四声,但在其他第四声音节的前面要改发第二声。例如:

The tone change of "不". Originally "不" is in the fourth tone, but when it is followed by another fourth tone *Hanzi*, it is read in the second tone. For example:

不是　不会　不贵　不去

"一"的变调。"一"的原调是第一声,但在在第一声、第二声和第三声音节的前面要改发第四声,在第四声音节的前面要改发第二声。例如:

The tone changes of "一". Originally "一" is in the first tone, but when it is followed by a syllable or *Hanzi* in the first, second or third tone, it is read in the fourth tone. When it is followed by a fourth tone syllable and *Hanzi*, it is read in the second tone. For example:

一 + 第一声:一天　一家　一生

一 + 第二声:一国　一名　一同

一 + 第三声:一场　一本　一体

一 + 第四声:一个　一向　一样

"一"在"一月"中仍发第一声。

However, "一" in "一月" keeps its original first tone.

1.4 "a, e, i"的读音。"a, e, i"都有不同的读音,下面举例说明。

Pronunciation of "a, e, i". "a, e, i" are pronounced differently and the following are some examples:

(1) a. "a"有不同的读音,但是都用字母"a"代表。试比较:

The letter "a" can be pronounced differently, but all are written as "a". Let's compare:

ta ma jia

tan san kan

tang zhang guang

(2) e. "e" 不同的读音,但是都用字母"e"代表。试比较:

The different pronunciations of letter "e" are all written as "e". Let's compare:

ge ke he

ye jie xie

(3) i. "i"有不同的读音,但是都用字母"i"代表。试比较:

The letter "i" can be pronounced differently, but all are written as "i". Let's compare:

ji qi xi

zhi chi shi ri

zi ci si

2. 汉语音节的书写 Spelling of Chinese syllables

2.1 书写规则。我们用汉语拼音书写汉语音节。用汉语拼音书写汉语音节有以下规则:

Spelling rules. *Hanyu Pinyin* are used to spell *Hanyu* syllables. The following rules should be observed to spell Chinese syllables:

(1)"i、in、ing"可以自成音节,自成音节时的写法是在前面加"y",写做"yi、yin、ying";其他以"i"开头的韵母也可以自成音节,自成音节时的写法是把"i"改为"y",写做"ya ye yao you yan yang yong"。写法改变后"i"的发音不变。

"i", "in" and "ing" each can be a syllable, then "y" should be added to them, i. e. they are written as "yi", "yin", "ying". While the final beginning with "i" can be also a syllable, then it should be changed to "y". They are written as "ya", "ye", "yao", "you", "yan", "yang", and "yong". The pronunciation of "i" remains the same.

(2)"ü、üe、üan、ün"可以自成音节,自成音节时的写法是在前面加"y",同时把"ü"改为"u",写做"yu、yue、yuan、yun"。它们前面有"j、q、x"作声母时,"ü、üe、üan、ün"中的"ü"也要改为"u"。写法改变后"ü"的发音不变。

"ü", "üe", "üan" and "ün" each can be a syllable, then "y" should be added to them, with the two dots over "ü" omitted. They are written as "yu", "yue", "yuan" and "yun". The two dots over "ü" in "ü", "üe", "üan" and "ün" are also omitted when they are preceded by the initials "j", "q" and "x". The pronunciation remains the same.

(3)"u"可以自成音节,自成音节时的写法是在前面加"w",写做"wu"。其他以"u"开头的韵母也可以自成音节,自成音节时要把"u"改为"w",写做"wa, wo, wai, wei, wan, wen, wang, weng"。写法改变后"u"的发音不变。

"u" can be a syllable itself, then "w" should be added to it, i.e. it should be written as "wu". While the initial beginning with "u" can be a syllable itself too, then "u" is changed to "w" and they are written as "wa", "wo", "wai", "wei", "wan", "wen", "wang" and "weng". The pronunciation of "u" remains the same.

(4)"iou、uei、uen"前面有声母时要写做"iu、ui、un","iu、ui、un"的实际读音还是"iou、uei、uen"。例如:

When they are preceded by an initial, "iou", "uei" and "uen" are written as "iu", "ui" and "un", which remain the same pronunciations as "iou, uei, uen". For example:

x+iou→xiu

g+uei→gui

d+uen→dun

2.2 声调符号(调号) The tone marks

汉语的音节用不同的声调符号标注声调。声调符号如下:

In writing, the tones in Chinese syllables are represented by different tone marks. The tone marks are as follows:

ā á ǎ à

以上字母a上面的符号依次代表第一声至第四声的声调符号。

The marks over the letter "a" indicate the first, the second, the third and the fourth tones respectively.

声调符号要标在元音或主要元音上,主要元音即开口度最大的元音。例如:

附录1 汉语音节的语音结构和书写方法

The tone marks are usually placed over the main final of a syllable, i. e. the one that is pronounced with wider aperture of the mouth. For example:

第一声：tāng　tiān
第二声：rén　méi
第三声：nǐ　niǎn
第四声：qù　quàn

轻声和轻声变调一般不标调号，半三声变调以及"一"和"不"的变调仍标原调。

Normally a neutral tone syllable goes without any tone mark. The half-third tone syllable, "一" and "不" are marked as they are originally pronounced.

附录 2　字词表
Appendix 2　Table of *zi* and *zi*-groups

字词表　Table of *Zi* and *zi*-groups

(说明:字词前面带"·"的是补充生词)

A

爱	(ài)	like; love; be fond of; keen on	(23)
爱吃		like eating	(23)
爱人	(àiren)	husband or wife	(23)
·爱国		love one's country; be patriotic	(23)
·爱好	(àihào)	take great pleasure in	(23)
·爱美		set great store by one's appearance	(23)
·爱面子		be concerned about face-saving	(23)
安	(ān)	peaceful; at ease	(8)
·安定		stable; quiet; settled	(28)

B

八	(bā)	eight	(1)
八折		80% of the original price; 20% discount	(24)
·八国		eight countries	(6)
爸	(bà)	pa; dad	(29)
爸爸	(bàba)	爸	(29)
吧	(ba)	a modal particle	(16)
白	(bái)	white	(26)
白酒		white spirit	(17)
白天		day (time between dawn to dusk)	(17)
白斩鸡		tender boiled chicken with a drop of soy sauce	(22)
·白菜		Chinese cabbage	(21)
·白日		white sun; day time	(17)
百	(bǎi)	hundred	(24)
办	(bàn)	do; handle; manage	(16)
办公		handle official business	(16)

附录2 字词表

办公室		office	(16)
办事		handle affairs; act; work	(27)
·办学		run a schoo	(16)
包	(bāo)	wrap; bag	(23)
包子	(bāozi)	steamed stuffed bun	(23)
饱	(bǎo)	have eaten to the full	(23)
饱了		be full; have eaten to the full	(23)
杯	(bēi)	cup; *a measure-zi*	(21)
杯子		cup	(21)
北	(běi)	north	(9)
北大		*short for* 北京大学	(9)
北方		north; the North	(23)
北京		Beijing	(9)
北京大学		Peking University	(9)
北京饭店		Beijing Hotel	(18)
北京人		a native of Beijing	(9)
北京市		Beijing municipality	(28)
辈	(bèi)	generation	(29)
本	(běn)	one's own; *a measure-zi*	(2)
本子	(běnzi)	notebook	(2)
·本国		one's own country	(6)
·本家		a distant relative with the same family name; a member of the same clan	(4)
·本来		original; at first	(11)
·本人		oneself; myself	(2)
·本身		itself; in itself	(4)
·本书		this book	(2)
比	(bǐ)	compare; contrast; than	(18)
比较		compare; fairly; comparatively	(18)
必	(bì)	certainly; surely; necessarily	(26)
必须		must; have to	(29)
便	(biàn)	convenient; handy; informal	(26)
病	(bìng)	illness; sickness; disease	(14)
病了		be ill	(14)
·病人		sick person; patient	(14)
补	(bǔ)	repair; mend	(28)
不	(bù)	no	(6)
不必		not necessarily	(26)
不长		be not long	(8)
不短		be not short	(8)

117

不对		be incorrect	(26)
不敢		not dare to do sth.	(17)
不高		be not tall	(14)
不贵		be not expensive	(11)
不过		but	(18)
不好		be not good	(6)
不会		can not (do sth.)	(6)
不久		soon; before long; not long after	(17)
不客气		no thanks; not at all	(16)
不看		do not read (see, watch)	(8)
不强		be not so strong	(28)
不少		be not so few; considerable; ample	(24)
不是		be not	(6)
不顺		be not so smooth	(26)
不太忙		be not so busy	(17)
不用		not needed	(13)
不远		be not far away	(8)
不在		be not (in,on) (a place)	(8)
不在家		be not at home	(8)
不重		be not so heavy	(28)
·不便		不方便	(26)
·不晚		be not late	(17)

C

菜	(cài)	vegetable; food; dish; course	(21)
菜单		menu	(24)
参	(cān)	participate	(29)
参加		join; take part in	(29)
餐	(cān)	food; meal	(24)
餐饮		food and drink	(24)
次	(cì)	time; secondary	(24)
·次数		number of times; frequency	(24)
从	(cóng)	follow; join; from	(19)
从…向…		go... from...	(19)
从…到…		from... to...	(19)

CH

茶	(chá)	tea	(21)
长	(cháng)	be long	(8)

附录2 字词表

长安街		Chang'an Street	(8)
长不长		be long or not	(8)
长久		prolonged; lasting	(17)
长寿		long life	(14)
长项		strong point	(27)
常	(cháng)	often	(14)
常常		常	(14)
尝	(cháng)	taste; have a taste of	(23)
尝尝	(chángchang)	have a taste of	(23)
场	(chǎng)	*a large place used for a particular purpose*	(8)
车	(chē)	vehicle	(19)
车站		stop; station; depot	(19)
成	(chéng)	accomplish; succeed	(28)
成功		success; successful	(28)
成为		become; turn into	(28)
·成就		achievement; accomplishment	(28)
·成双		form a pair	(28)
·成语		idiom	(28)
吃	(chī)	eat	(17)
吃饱		have eaten one's fill	(23)
吃饱了		饱了	(23)
吃得太多		to have eaten too much	(24)
吃饭		eat; have a meal	(17)
吃午饭		have lunch	(18)
·吃不下		be unable to eat any more	(17)

D

打	(dǎ)	do; beat; strike; hit	(16)
打八折		charge 80% of the original price; give 20%	(24)
打包		ale; pack	(23)
打的	(dǎdī)	take a taxi	(19)
打电话		make a telephone call	(16)
打折		sell at a discount; give a discount	(24)
·打工		do manual work	(26)
·打算	(dǎsuan)	intend; plan; think of; consideration	(28)
·打听		ask about; inquire about	(27)
大	(dà)	be big; be large	(1)
大家		everybody; all (people)	(4)
大忙人		busy bee	(17)

119

大门		front door; gate	(8)
大米		rice	(23)
大学		college; university	(9)
大学生		college student(s)	(9)
·大便		human excrement; shit	(26)
·大海		海	(9)
·大人	(dàren)	adult; grown-up	(1)
·大人	(dàrén)	*old* Your Excellency or His Excellency	(1)
单	(dān)	bill; list; single	(24)
·单位		unit	(24)
担	(dān)	carry on a shoulder pole; take on; undertake	(29)
担心		worry; feel anxious; fear	(29)
导	(dǎo)	lead; guide	(17)
·导师		tutor; teacher; guide of a great cause	
到	(dào)	arrive; reach	(14)
道	(dào)	way; road; path; say; talk; speak	(18)
的	(de)	*a particle-zi*	(4)
得	(de)	*a structural particle*	(24)
地	(de)	*a structural particle*	(29)
等	(děng)	wait; and so on	(26)
等人		wait for a person	(26)
等一会儿		wait a minute	(26)
等于		equal to; equivalent to	(27)
的	(dī)	*here is the short form for* "的士" (dīshì: taxi)	(19)
点	(diǎn)	o'clock; point; drop; dot; put a dot	(18)
点钟		o'clock	(19)
点心	(diǎnxin)	refreshments	(23)
·点儿		a bit; a little	(21)
点	(diǎn)	select; choose; order	(21)
点菜		order dishes (in a restaurant)	(21)
电	(diàn)	electricity	(16)
电话		telephone	(16)
电话号码		telephone number	(16)
电视		television	(28)
电视机		television set	(28)
电子	(diànzǐ)	electron	(27)
店	(diàn)	shop; store	(18)
定	(dìng)	certainly; definitely; still; stable	(18)
东	(dōng)	east	(19)
东方		the east; the East; the Orient	(23)

东京		Tokyo (capital of Japan)	(19)
东面		the east	(19)
·东南		southeast	(19)
·东西	(dōngxi)	thing; stuff	(19)
董	(dǒng)	supervise; direct	(27)
董事		director	(27)
董事长		chairman of the board	(27)
都	(dōu)	all; both; every	(12)
豆	(dòu)	pod-bearing plant or its seeds; bean	(22)
豆腐	(dòufu)	bean curd	(22)
短	(duǎn)	short; brief	(28)
对	(duì)	correct; right; treat; be directed at	(26)
对得起		treat fairly; do justice to	(26)
对不起		sorry; excuse me	(26)
多	(duō)	many; much; more	(19)
多大		how old (asking the age)	(19)
多长		how long	(19)
多长时间		how long time	(19)
多少	(duōshao)	how many; how much	(24)
多少钱		how much	(24)
多数		majority; major	(23)
多谢		many thanks	(19)

E

儿	(ér)	son	(4)
儿子	(érzi)	son	(4)
儿女		son(s) and daughter(s)	(4)
二	(èr)	two	(1)
二十		twenty	(1)
二十分钟		twenty minutes	(19)
二十一		twenty-one	(1)
二月		February	(7)

F

发	(fā)	give out; distribute; produce; develop; expand	(28)
发生		happen; occur; arise; take place	(28)
·发奖		award prizes; present prizes	(28)
·发现		find; discover; detect; become aware of; discovery	(28)
烦	(fán)	be annoyed; be tired of	(17)

饭	(fàn)	cooked rice or other cereals; meal	(17)
饭店		hotel; restaurant	(18)
饭食		food	(23)
·饭菜		meal	(21)
方	(fāng)	direction; square; place	(23)
方便		convenient	(26)
·方面		aspect	(23)
·方向		direction; orientation	(23)
非	(fēi)	oppose; find fault with	(14)
非常		very; extremely; highly	(14)
非常高兴		be extremely glad	(14)
非常快乐		be extremely happy	(14)
非正式		不是正式的	(29)
飞	(fēi)	fly	(4)
飞机		air plane	(14)
分	(fēn)	minute; divide	(19)
分公司		branch of a company	(19)
分钟		minute	(19)
·分离		leave each other; separate; part	(19)
夫	(fū)	husband; man; person engaged in manual labor	(28)
夫人	(fūren)	a lady of high rank; Madame; Mrs.; the wife of a high official	(28)
服	(fú)	serve	(21)
服务		serve; give service to	(21)
服务员		attendant; waiter	(21)
腐	(fǔ)	rotten; any bean product	(22)
辅	(fǔ)	assist; supplement	(17)
辅导		coach; give guidance in study or training	(17)
父	(fù)	father	(13)
父亲		father	(13)
·父母		father and mother	(13)
·父女		father and daughter(s)	(13)
·父子	(fùzǐ)	father and son(s)	(13)

G

该	(gāi)	ought to be; should be	(18)
敢	(gǎn)	dare; be brave enough	(17)
·敢想敢说		dare to think and dare to act	(17)
·敢说敢做		dare to speak and dare to act	(17)
感	(gǎn)	feel; sense; be aware	(29)
感谢		thank; be thankful; be grateful	(29)

·感到		feel; sense	(29)
·感想		impressions; reflections; thought	(29)
刚	(gāng)	just; exactly; precisely	(27)
刚刚		刚	(27)
高	(gāo)	be tall; be high	(14)
高兴		be glad; be happy; be cheerful	(14)
高兴死了		be extremely happy	(29)
个	(gè)	*a measure-zi*	(1)
给	(gěi)	give; for; to	(16)
工	(gōng)	work; worker	(9)
工人		worker	(9)
工作		work; job	(9)
工作很忙		be very busy at work	(17)
·工夫	(gōngfu)	time; skill	(28)
公	(gōng)	public; state-owned; collective	(9)
公家		the public	(9)
公共		public; common	(19)
公共汽车		bus	(19)
公路		highway	(26)
公司		company; corporation	(9)
·公司项目		company's project	(27)
·公式		formula	(29)
·公文		official document	(9)
·公务		public affairs; official business	(21)
·公务员		public servant; civil servant; civil service	(21)
功	(gōng)	achievement; merit; effect; success	(28)
共	(gōng)	common; general; altogether; in all	(19)
共计		add up to; amount to	(24)
·共同		common; shared; jointly	(19)
够	(gòu)	enough; sufficient; adequate	(22)
顾	(gù)	turn round and look at; take into consideration	(29)
关	(guān)	shut; close; concern; involve	(18)
关门		close (the door)	(18)
关系		connections; relationship	(18)
关心		be concerned with; care for	(29)
关于		concerning; about; with regard to	(27)
关照		look after; take care of	(29)
广	(guǎng)	wide; broad; vast; extensive	(8)
广场		square	(8)

附录 2　字词表

广大		vast; wide	(8)
贵	(guì)	expensive; costly; noble	(11)
贵客		honoured guest	(29)
贵姓		(may I ask) your name (*a polite form for asking one's surname*)	(11)
·贵国		a polite form for "your country"	(11)
国	(guó)	country; nation; state	(6)
·国家		country	(6)
·国家项目		national project	(27)
过	(guò)	cross; pass	(8)
过路		pass by one's way	(26)
过去		go over; past by; (in or of) the past	(8)
·过年		celebrate the New Year	(8)
过	(guò)	go beyond	(11)
过奖		overpraise	(11)

H

还	(hái)	also; still	(16)
还…没有…(呢)		have not (done sth.) yet	(16)
还是		or (used in questions)	(21)
还要		also need	(17)
海	(hǎi)	sea	(9)
海上		at sea; on the sea	(9)
·海关		customs	(18)
韩	(hán)	Han (*a surname*)	(12)
韩国		the South Korea	(12)
·韩元		Korean won	(24)
汉	(hàn)	(Hàn) the Han nationality	(6)
汉语		Hanyu (the Han language; Chinese language)	(6)
汉语水平		Chinese language proficiency	(28)
汉字		*Hanzi* (Sinogram; Sinograph)	(12)
好	(hǎo)	good; well; nice	(3)
好不好		be good or not	(6)
好吃	(hǎochī)	be delicious	(17)
好久		很久	(17)
好久不见		have not met with each other for a long time	(17)
好像		seem; be like	(18)
好心		kind-hearted	(23)
·好人		a good (or nice) person	(3)
·好书		a nice book	(3)

号	(hào)	date; number	(7)
号码		number	(16)
喝	(hē)	drink	(21)
喝茶		drink tea	(21)
喝咖啡		drink coffee	(21)
和	(hé)	and	(4)
·和平		peaceful; tranquil; peace	(28)
合	(hé)	close; come together; add up to	(27)
合同	(hétong)	contract	(27)
合作		cooperate; cooperation; work together; collaborate	(27)
合作项目		cooperation project	(27)
·合计		amount to; total	(27)
贺	(hè)	congratulate; celebrate	(27)
很	(hěn)	very	(4)
很长		be very long	(8)
很短		be very short	(28)
很高		be very tall	(14)
很贵		be very expensive	(11)
很好		be very good (well; nice)	(4)
很久		be very long	(17)
很近		be very close	(18)
很快乐		be very happy	(14)
很忙		be very busy	(17)
很强		be very powerful	(28)
很少		be very little	(24)
很远		be very far away	(8)
很重		be very heavy	(28)
红	(hóng)	be red	(21)
红茶		black tea	(21)
红酒		wine	(21)
红烧		braise in soy sauce	(22)
回	(huí)	go (or come) back; turn round	(14)
回国		go (or come) back to one's own country	(14)
回家		go (or come) home	(14)
回来		come back	(14)
回美国		go (or come) back to the United States	(14)
回去		go back	(14)
后	(hòu)	behind; back; after; afterwards	(29)
后门		back door (or gate)	(29)
后年		the year after next	(29)

后天		the day after tomorrow	(29)
·后方		behind; at the back	(29)
·后来		afterwards; later	(29)
·后人		later generations	(29)
候	(hòu)	hour time; wait	(8)
互	(hù)	mutually	(28)
互利		mutual benefit; of mutual benefit	(28)
话	(huà)	word; talk; speak about	(16)
欢	(huān)	joyous; merry	(21)
欢迎		welcome	(26)
会	(huì)	know (how to do); can; be able to; be good at	(6)
会不会		if know (how to do)	(6)
会说		can speak	(6)
会	(huì)	meet; meeting	(11)
会见		meet; meet with	(11)
会客		receive a visitor or guest	(26)
会客室		reception room	(26)
会	(huì)	meeting; party; association; society	(26)
会谈		talk; negotiation	(27)
会议		meeting; conference	(27)
会议室		meeting room	(27)
惠	(huì)	favor; kindness; benefit	(24)

J

机	(jī)	machine; engine; chance	
·机会		chance; opportunity	(14)
鸡	(jī)	chicken	(22)
几	(jǐ)	how many; several; some; a few	(2)
几本书		how many books	(2)
几点		what time is it	(18)
几个		how many	(2)
几个本子		how many notebooks	(2)
几个人		how many people; a few people	(2)
几个小时		how many hours; a few hours	(8)
几个月		how many months	(7)
几号		what date is it	(7)
几位		how many people	(12)
几月		which month	(7)
几月几号		what date is it	(17)

附录2 字词表

几月几日		几月几号	(7)
计	(jì)	count; calculate	(24)
计算		count; calculate	(28)
计算机		computer	(28)
加	(jiā)	add; plus; put in	(29)
·加强		strengthen; intensify; enhance; reinforce	(29)
家	(jiā)	home; family; household	(4)
家常		the daily life of a family	(22)
家常豆腐		homely tofu	(22)
·家常菜		home cooking	(22)
·家常饭		homely food; simple meal	(22)
·家常话		small talk; chitchat	(22)
·家父		my father	
·家母		my mother	(13)
间	(jiān)	within a definite time or space; between; *a measure-zi*	(18)
见	(jiàn)	see; meet with; catch sight of	(8)
见到		meet with	
见过		have met; have seen	(8)
见面		meet with	(19)
件	(jiàn)	letter; document; *a measure-zi*	(27)
建	(jiàn)	build; construct; establish; set up	(7)
建成		succeed in building	(28)
健	(jiàn)	healthy; strong	(14)
健康		health; healthy; physique; physical condition	(14)
奖	(jiǎng)	praise	(11)
饺	(jiǎo)	a kind of dumpling	(23)
饺子	(jiǎozi)	dumpling (with meat and vegetable stuffing)	(23)
叫	(jiào)	call; be called; ask	(7)
叫马阳		be named Ma Yang	(7)
叫	(jiao)	order	(23)
叫点心		order refreshments	(23)
教	(jiào)	teach; instruct; religion	(12)
教授		professor; teach; instruct	(12)
教学		teach; teaching	(12)
教师		teacher	(13)
较	(jiào)	compare; contrast	(18)
街	(jiē)	street	(8)
接	(jiē)	receive; answer	(16)
接电话		answer the phone	(16)
结	(jié)	settle; finish; conclude	(24)

127

	结账		settle accounts; square accounts	(24)
	·结合		combine; identify	(27)
姐		(jiě)	elder sister	(12)
	姐姐	(jiějie)	姐	(12)
介		(jiè)	be situated between; interpose	(12)
	介绍		introduce; presentation	(12)
今		(jīn)	modern; present-day; now; today	(7)
	今年		this year	(8)
	今天		today	(7)
斤		(jīn)	a unit of weight, equivalent to 0.5 kilogram	(23)
近		(jìn)	be near; be close to	(18)
京		(jīng)	capital (of a country); Jing (*short for Beijing*)	(9)
经		(jīng)	undergo; pass through	(9)
	经过		pass; through; process	(23)
	经理		manager	(9)
井		(jǐng)	well	(21)
九		(jiǔ)	9	(2)
	九十		90	(2)
	九十九		99	(2)
久		(jiǔ)	be long (time)	(17)
	久等		wait for a long time	(27)
酒		(jiǔ)	alcoholic beverage; wine	(21)
	·酒菜		food and drink	(21)
	·酒店		wineshop; hotel	(21)
	·酒饭		drink and food	(21)
就		(jiù)	then; soon; in that case	(13)
	就职		accession; take up an appointment; assume office	(29)
	·就餐		*formal* dine; have a meal	(24)
句		(jù)	sentence	(29)
	句子		句	(29)

K

咖啡		(kāfēi)	coffee	(21)
开		(kāi)	open; start; operate; boil	(26)
	开车		drive a car	(26)
	开发		develop; exploit	(28)
	·开发市场		develop the market	(28)
	开会		hold or attend a meeting	(26)
	开门		open the door	(26)
	开水		boiled water	(26)

开玩笑		crack a joke; make fun of	(29)
开学		school opens; term begins	(26)
看	(kàn)	see; look at; watch; read (silently); call on	(8)
看得起		have a good opinion of; think highly of	(26)
看不起		look down upon	(26)
看不看		read (see, watch) or not	(8)
看见		catch sight of	(8)
看马建		call on Ma Jian; visit Ma Jian	(8)
看书		read (silently) book(s)	(8)
看望		call on; visit; see	(28)
·看病		(of a doctor) see a patient; (of a patient) see or consult a doctor	(14)
康	(kāng)	well-being; health	(14)
烤	(kǎo)	roast; bake	(22)
烤鸭		roast duck	(22)
可	(kě)	can; may	(16)
可以		may; can; be able to	(16)
·可能		possible; maybe	(19)
·可是		but	(16)
客	(kè)	guest	(16)
客气	(kèqi)	polite; modest	(16)
客人	(kèren)	visitor; guest; guest (at a hotel, etc.)	(16)
口	(kǒu)	mouth; *a measure-zi*	(4)
快	(kuài)	quick; fast; happy	(14)
快乐		happy	(14)

L

来	(lái)	come	(11)
来了		be coming; have (has) come; came	(13)
老	(lǎo)	old	(13)
老年人		老人	(13)
老人		old man or woman	(13)
老朋友		old friend(s)	(13)
老师		teacher	(13)
老王		old Wang	(13)
乐	(lè)	happy; cheerful; joyful; be glad to	(14)
了	(le)	*a particle*	(13)
累	(lèi)	be tired	(14)
离	(lí)	leave; be away from; part from	(19)
里	(lǐ)	in; inside	(22)

里面		inside; interior	(22)
理	(lǐ)	manage; run; reason; logic	(9)
鲤	(lǐ)	carp	(22)
鲤鱼		carp	(22)
力	(lì)	force; strength; power; ability	(28)
利	(lì)	benefits; interests	(28)
凉	(liáng)	cool; cold	(22)
凉菜		cold dish	(22)
·凉快	(liángkuai)	nice and cool	(22)
两	(liǎng)	2	(2)
两本书		2 books	(2)
两点钟		two o'clock	(19)
两个本子		2 notebooks	(2)
两个人		2 people	(2)
两个星期		2 weeks	(7)
两个月		2 months	(7)
两周		two weeks	(26)
·两国		two countries	(6)
料	(liào)	material; stuff	(21)
林	(lín)	forest; Lin (*a surname*)	(12)
林小姐		Miss Lin	(12)
林正美		Lin Zhengmei (*the name of a person*)	(12)
零	(líng)	zero	(24)
六	(liù)	six	(1)
六月一号		June the first	(7)
六月一日		六月一号	(7)
龙	(lóng)	dragon	(21)
龙井(茶)		Longjing tea	(21)
路	(lù)	road; way	(26)
路过		pass by or through (a place)	(26)
路上		on the road	(26)
·路面		road surface; pavement	(26)
乱	(luàn)	in disorder	(29)
绿	(lǜ)	green	(21)
绿茶		green tea	(21)

M

妈	(mā)	母亲	(17)
妈妈		妈	(17)
麻	(má)	rough	(17)

附录 2　字词表

麻烦	(máfan)	troublesome; inconvenient	(17)
马	(mǎ)	horse;（Mǎ）*a family name*	(4)
马飞(名)		Ma Fei (*name of a person*)	(4)
马飞的		Ma Fei's	(4)
马飞家		Ma Fei's home (family)	(4)
马飞先生		Mr. Ma Fei	(6)
马家		Ma's Family	(4)
马建		Ma Jian (*name of a person*)	(7)
马太太		Mrs.Ma	(4)
马先生		Mr.Ma	(6)
马阳		Ma Yang (*name of a person*)	(7)
码	(mǎ)	*a sign or thing indicating number;* yard (yd.)	(16)
吗	(ma)	*a question zi*	(3)
买	(mǎi)	buy; purchase	(24)
买单		pay for the bill	(24)
买东西		buy things	(24)
忙	(máng)	be busy	(17)
么	(me)	*a particle-zi used to form a zi-group*	(7)
没	(méi)	not (do); without; not have; there is not	(3)
没关系		it doesn't matter	(18)
没见过		have not met	(8)
没看		have not read (see, watch)	(8)
没看见		have not catch sight of	(8)
没去过		have not been to	(8)
没想到		have not expect; never expect	(17)
没有		do not have; there be not; be without	(3)
没有本子		do not have notebook(s); there is (are) no notebook(s)	(3)
没有书		do not have book(s); there is (are) no book(s)	(3)
美	(měi)	beautiful; pretty;（Měi）short for "美国"	(12)
美国		the United States (U.S.A.)	(12)
·美元		US dollar; American dollar	(24)
门	(mén)	door; gate	(8)
们	(men)	*a particle-zi used to form a plural*	(3)
米	(mǐ)	rice; shelled or husked seed (usu.edible)	(23)
米饭		cooked rice	(23)
面		face; surface; side	(19)
·面向		turn one's face to; face	(19)
·面了		outer part; face	(19)
面	(miàn)	wheat flour	(23)
面包		bread	(23)

面食		food made from flour	(23)
面条		noodle	(23)
免	(miǎn)	dispense with	(11)
免贵		dispense with "贵" (guì: noble) before surname	(11)
名	(míng)	name	(12)
名单		name list	(24)
名字		name	(12)
·名次		position in a name list	(24)
明	(míng)	bright; brilliant; light	(7)
明年		next year	(8)
明天		tomorrow	(7)
·明日		明天	(7)
·明月		bright moon	(7)
母	(mǔ)	mother	(13)
母亲		mother	(13)
·母子	(mǔzi)	mother and son(s)	(13)
·母女		mother and daughter(s)	(13)
木	(mù)	wood; tree	(11)
目	(mù)	eye; item	(27)
项目		item; project	
合作项目		cooperation project; joint project	

N

哪	(nǎ)	where	(8)
哪儿	(nǎr)	where	(8)
哪能		how can; how could	
那	(nà)	that	(19)
那儿		there	(18)
那里	(nàli)	那儿	(22)
那样		of that kind; like that; such; so	(18)
南	(nán)	south	(19)
南方		south; the South	(23)
南京		Nanjing (*the capital of Jiangsu Province*)	(19)
南面		south; the south	(19)
·南门		south gate	(19)
男	(nán)	man; male	(26)
男的		男人	(26)
男人		man	(26)
男朋友		boyfriend	(26)

呢	(ne)	a modal particle	(16)
能	(néng)	can; be able to	(19)
能到		can arrive	
能力		ability; capability; capacity	(28)
你	(nǐ)	you (*single*)	(3)
你的		yours	(4)
你好		how do you do	(3)
你家		your family (home)	(4)
你们		you (*plural*)	(3)
年	(nián)	year	(8)
年年		every year	(8)
您	(nín)	a polite form for "你"	(14)
您好		how do you do	(14)
女	(nǚ)	female; daughter	(4)
女儿	(nǚér)	daughter	(4)
·女人		woman; women	(4)

P

判		distinguish; judge	(27)
朋	(péng)	fellow disciples	
朋友	(péngyou)	friend(s)	(13)
啤酒	(píjiǔ)	beer	(21)
便宜	(piányi)	cheap; inexpensive	
平	(píng)	flat; level; smooth; make it a level	(28)
·平等		equal; equality	
瓶	(píng)	bottle; vase; jar; *a measure-zi*	(21)
瓶子	(píngzi)	bottle	(21)

Q

七	(qī)	seven	(2)
七十		70	(2)
七十七		77	(2)
期	(qī)	period of time; phase	(7)
期满		expired; come to an end	(29)
起		rise; *up to a certain standard*	(26)
气	(qì)	air; gas; breath	(16)
·气候		climate	(16)
汽	(qì)	vapour; steam	(19)
汽车		automobile; motor vehicle; car	(19)

千	(qiān)	thousand	(24)
前	(qián)	front; before	(23)
前年		year before last	(23)
前天		the day before yesterday	(23)
·前方		ahead; in front	(23)
·前面		in front; forward	(23)
钱	(qián)	money; cash; coin	(24)
钱包		wallet; purse	(23)
亲	(qīn)	parent; kin; relative	(23)
·亲人		one's parent; spouse; children	(13)
青	(qīng)	green; black; blue	(22)
青菜		green vegetable	(22)
·青年		youth; young people	(22)
清	(qīng)	clear; explicit; distinct	(22)
清蒸		steam in clear soup (usu.without soy sauce)	(22)
情	(qíng)	feeling; situation	(29)
请	(qǐng)	invite; request; please; ask	(13)
请问		may I ask	(19)
请坐		please sit down	(13)
·请客		invite guest to dinner; treat	(16)
·请客吃饭		invite guest to dinner	(17)
去	(qù)	go	(7)
去过		have been to	(8)
去年		last year	(8)

R

让	(ràng)	allow; let; give way; give in; yield	(27)
让开		step aside; get out of the way	
让路		make way for sb.or sth.	(27)
热	(rè)	be hot	(22)
热菜		hot dish	(22)
热情		warm; warmth	
热情地		warmly	(29)
人	(rén)	people; person	(1)
人工		man made	(9)
·人口		population	(4)
认	(rèn)	recognize; know	(13)
认识	(rènshi)	know; understand; recognize	(13)
日	(rì)	the sun; date; day	(7)
日本		Japan	(7)

日本人		Japanese (people)	(7)
日语		Japanese (language)	(7)
日元		Japanese yen	(24)
·日期		date	(7)
·日子	(rìzi)	day; date; days; time; life	(7)
肉	(ròu)	meat; pork	(22)
软	(ruǎn)	soft	(27)
软件		software	(27)

S

三	(sān)	three	(1)
三木		name of a person	(11)
三十		thirty	(1)
三十二		thirty-two	(1)
三天		three days	(1)
三月八号		March the eighth	(7)
三月八日		三月八号	(7)
散	(sàn)	break up; distribute; scatter	(27)
散会		(of a meeting) be over; break up	(27)
·散开		disperse	(27)
·散心		keep from worrying; relieve one's boredom	(27)
司	(sī)	manage; take charge of	(9)
司长		director of a department (in a ministry)	(27)
·司机		driver	(16)
死	(sǐ)	die; be dead; to the death	(29)
四	(sì)	4	(2)
四口人		four family members	(4)
四十		40	(2)
四十四		44	(2)
算	(suàn)	calculate; estimate	(28)
·算账		do or work out accounts	(28)

SH

沙发	(shāfā)	sofa	(29)
上	(shàng)	upper; upward; go up; go to; mount; board; get on	(9)
上海		Shanghai (China's largest city)	(9)
上次		last time	(24)
上个月		last month	(9)
上午		morning	(18)

上星期		last week	(9)
上学		go to school	(9)
上学年		last school year	(9)
上学期		last term; last semester	(9)
上周		last week	(27)
·上街		go to the street; go shopping	(9)
·上去		go up; move from a lower level to a higher level	(9)
烧	(shāo)	roast; braise; burn	(22)
·烧鸡		roast chicken	(22)
·烧烤		barbecue	(22)
少	(shǎo)	be few; be little	(24)
绍	(shào)	carry on; continue	(12)
设	(shè)	set up; form	(27)
设计		design; plan	(27)
设计水平		level of design	(28)
谁	(shéi)	who	(7)
身	(shēn)	body	(4)
身体		body; health	(4)
身体很好		be in good health	(4)
身体怎么样		how is (one's) health	(18)
什	(shén)	what	(7)
什么		what	(7)
什么人		what kind of people	(7)
什么时候		when; at what time	(8)
什么书		what book	(7)
生	(shēng)	pupil; student; be born; give birth to	(6)
生日		birthday	(7)
·生病		fall ill	(14)
·生气		get angry	(16)
师	(shī)	teacher	(13)
师母		wife of one's teacher or master	(14)
十	(shí)	ten	(1)
十二点		twelve o'clock	(18)
十二个月		twelve months	(7)
十九		19	(2)
十七		17	(2)
十四		14	(2)
十五		15	(2)
十一		eleven	(1)
十月一号		October the first	(7)

附录 2 字词表

十月一日		十月一号	(7)
时	(shí)	time; fixed time; hour	(8)
时候		moment; (the duration of) time; (a point in) time	(8)
时间		time	(18)
食	(shí)	food; meal; eat	(23)
式	(shì)	style; type; fashion	(29)
市	(shì)	market; municipality	(28)
市场		marketplace; market	(28)
·市场开发		market development	(28)
市面		market	(28)
市长		mayor	(28)
室	(shì)	room	(16)
事	(shì)	matter; affair; thing; business	(27)
·事情		事	(29)
视	(shì)	look; view; look upon	(28)
实	(shí)	reality; actuality; fact	(12)
实习		practice	(12)
实习期		the period of practice	(29)
·实现		realize; achieve; bring about	(23)
识	(shí)	know; knowledge	(13)
·实在		honest	(12)
是	(shì)	be; yes	(6)
是不是		yes or no	(6)
·是非		right and wrong; truth and falsehood	(14)
手	(shǒu)	hand	(16)
手机		mobile phone; hand phone	(16)
寿	(shòu)	life; long life	(11)
授	(shòu)	pass on knowledge; confer; give	(12)
书	(shū)	book	(2)
书包		schoolbag	(23)
·书本		book	(2)
·书店		book store	(18)
数	(shù)	number; figure	(23)
·数字		numeral; figure	(23)
双	(shuāng)	even; double	(28)
双方		both sides; two parties	(28)
双赢		win-win	(28)
水	(shuǐ)	water	(26)
水不开		the water is not boiled	(26)
水开了		the water is boiled	(26)

137

水没开		the water has not been boiled	(26)
水平		standard; level	(28)
顺	(shùn)	agreeable; obey; yield to	(26)
顺便		incidentally; in passing	(26)
顺路		on the way; direct route	(26)
说	(shuō)	speak; say; talk	(6)
说话		speak; talk	(16)
说起		talk about	(27)
说什么		what to say	(7)
·说明		explain; show; prove; explanation	(7)
·说明书		(a booklet of) directions	(7)

T

他	(tā)	he	(3)
他们		they (*for male*)	(3)
他们家		their family (home)	(4)
她	(tā)	she	(3)
她们		they (*for female*)	(3)
太	(tài)	too; excessively	(1)
太大		too big; too large	(1)
太贵		be too expensive	(11)
太太	(tàitai)	Mrs.; Madam; lady; wife	(4)
太阳		the sun	(7)
谈	(tán)	talk; speak; chat	(27)
谈成		succeed in negotiation	(28)
谈话		conversation; talk; chat	(27)
谈判		negotiate; talk; negotiation	(27)
题	(tí)	topic; write; inscribe	(26)
·题字		write; inscribe	(26)
·题目		title; subject; topic; exercise problems; examination items	(27)
体	(tǐ)	body	(4)
替	(tì)	replace; substitute	(17)
天	(tiān)	the sky; the heavens; day	(1)
天安门		Tian'an Men	(8)
天安门广场		Tian'an Men Square	(8)
天大		As large as the heavens; extremely big	(1)
太好了		wonderful; excellent	(18)
天明		daybreak; dawn	(7)
天天		every day	(1)
·天气		weather	(16)

·天儿凉		it's cold	(22)
·天儿热		it's hot	(22)
条	(tiáo)	*a measure-zi*	(22)
一条鱼		one fish	(22)
·条约		treaty; pact	(26)
听	(tīng)	listen; hear	(27)
听说		be told; 听和说	(27)
同	(tóng)	same; alike; do together; share in common	(11)
同学		classmate; schoolmate	(11)

W

玩	(wán)	play; have fun; amuse oneself	(29)
玩儿		玩	(29)
玩笑		joke	(29)
晚	(wǎn)	evening; night; night time; late (for sth.)	(17)
晚会		evening party	(26)
晚上	(wǎnshang)	evening; (at) night	(17)
·晚安		good evening; good night	(17)
·晚辈		the younger generation; one's juniors	(29)
·晚饭		supper; dinner	(17)
·晚了		be late (for sth.)	(17)
·晚年		old age; one's later years	(17)
碗	(wǎn)	bowl; bowl-like vessel or object	(23)
王	(wáng)	king; (Wáng) *a surname*	(11)
王同		Wang Tong *(full name of a person)*	(11)
望	(wàng)	look or gaze into the distance; call on; pay a visit	(28)
位	(wèi)	location; *a measure-zi*	(12)
为	(wéi)	do; act; be; mean	(26)
文	(wén)	writing; literary language	(9)
·文本		text; version	(9)
·文人		man of letters; scholar	(9)
·文学		literature	(9)
问	(wèn)	ask	(17)
问好		say hello to	(17)
问人		ask	(18)
问题		problem; question	(26)
·问安		(*usu.to elders*) pay one's respects; wish sb.good health	(17)
我	(wǒ)	I	(3)
我的		my; mine	(4)
我家		my family (home)	(4)

	我们	we	(3)
五	(wǔ)	5	(2)
	五十	50	(2)
	五十五	55	(2)
	五月	May	(7)
	五月一号	May the first	(7)
	五月一日	五月一号	(7)
午	(wǔ)	noon; midday	(18)
	午饭	中饭	(18)
	·午安	good noon	(18)
务	(wù)	be engaged in	(21)

X

西	(xī)	west	(19)
	西安	Xi'an (*the capital of Shanxi province*)	(19)
	西餐	Western-style food; Western food	(24)
	西方	the west; the West	(23)
	西面	the west	(19)
	·西北	northwest	(19)
希	(xī)	hope	(28)
	希望	hope; wish; expect	(28)
息	(xī)	cease; stop	(29)
习	(xí)	practise; exercise; review	(9)
喜	(xǐ)	like; happy; delighted; a happy event (esp.wedding)	(21)
	喜欢	(xǐhuan) like; love; be fond of	(21)
	·喜酒	wine drunk at a wedding feast; wedding feast	(21)
系	(xì)	relate to; bear on	(18)
下	(xià)	come or go down; under; below; lower; next (here is used as) *a measure–zi*	(12)
	下次	next time	(24)
	下回	下次	(24)
	下午	afternoon	(18)
先	(xiān)	in advance; first; earlier	(6)
	先生	(xiānsheng) teacher; Mister; gentle man; sir	(6)
现	(xiàn)	show; appear; reveal	(23)
	现在	now; nowadays; currently	(23)
想	(xiǎng)	think; want	(14)
	想到了	have expected	(14)
向	(xiàng)	direction; turn towards; to	(17)

附录2 字词表

向…问好		say hello to sb.	(17)
·向前		towards the front; forward	(23)
·向前看		looking forward	(23)
·向西		towards west	(19)
项	(xiàng)	nape (of the neck); *a measure-zi*	(27)
项目		item; project	(27)
像	(xiàng)	be like	(12)
消	(xiāo)	disappear	(29)
消气		cool down; be mollified	
消息	(xiāoxi)	information	(29)
小	(xiǎo)	be small; be little; be young	(6)
小儿子		younger son	(6)
小姐		a young (unmarried) lady; Miss	(12)
小时		hour	(8)
小心		careful	(23)
·小便		urinate; piss	(26)
·小气	(xiǎoqi)	stingy; mean	(16)
·小人		a small man	(6)
·小时候		childhood; early youth	(8)
·小说		novel; fiction	(6)
笑	(xiào)	smile; laugh	(29)
·笑话		joke; jest	(29)
协	(xié)	aid; assist	(27)
协议		agree on; agreement	(27)
协议书		agreement	(27)
谢	(xiè)	thank; (Xie) *a surname*	(11)
谢谢	(xièxie)	thanks	(11)
谢谢你		thank you	(11)
心	(xīn)	heart	(23)
心情		frame of mind; mood	(29)
星	(xīng)	star	(7)
星期		week	(7)
星期几		what day	(7)
星期一		Monday	(7)
星期二		Tuesday	(7)
星期六		Saturday	(7)
星期天		Sunday	(7)
星期日		星期天	(7)
姓	(xìng)	(*one's surname*) be	(11)
姓王		(one's) surname is Wang	(11)

141

·姓什么		what (one's) surname be	(11)
幸	(xìng)	fortunate; lucky	(11)
幸会		*pol.* very pleased to meet you (*a rather formal greeting*)	(11)
兴	(xìng)	interest; excitement; mood or desire to do something	(14)
须	(xū)	beard; must; have to	(29)
·须要		须	(29)
·须知		one should know that	(29)
学	(xué)	study; learn; school; knowledge; theory	(9)
学汉语		learn Chinese language	(9)
学年		school year	(9)
学期		school term; semester	(9)
学生	(xuésheng)	student; pupil; follower	(9)
学习		study; learn	(9)
学习汉语		学汉语	(9)

Y

鸭	(yā)	duck	(22)
言	(yán)	speech; remark; say; talk	(11)
言语		speech; word; say	(11)
阳	(yáng)	the sun	(7)
样	(yàng)	appearance; shape; sample; model	(18)
样式		pattern; style; type; fashion	(29)
·样子	(yàngzi)	appearance; shape; sample	(18)
要	(yào)	must; need; want; be going to; be about to	(17)
要是		if	(19)
也	(yě)	also; too	(3)
也不会		also can not (do sth.)	(6)
也没有		also do not have	(3)
也有		also have	(3)
业	(yè)	occupation; profession	(9)
一	(yī)	one	(1)
一辈子		all one's life; life time	(29)
一本书		one book	(2)
一定		definitely; inevitably; necessarily	(28)
一个本子		one notebook	(2)
一个人		one person	(1)
一个碗		one bowl	(23)
一个小时		one hour	(8)
一会儿		a little while	(13)
1949年		(in) the year of 1949	(8)

一句话		(have) a word	(29)
一年多		one year and more	(29)
一天		one day	(1)
一起		together	(29)
一碗		one bowl of	(23)
一碗米饭		one bowl of cooked rice	(23)
一下		once; in a short while	(12)
·一点儿		a bit; a little	(21)
·一共		altogether; in all	(19)
·一样		the same; alike	(18)
宜	(yí)	suitable; appropriate; desirable	(24)
已	(yǐ)	already	(23)
已经		already	(23)
以	(yǐ)	with; by means of; in order to	(16)
以后		after; afterwards; later on	(29)
以来		since	(29)
以前		before; previously	(23)
以为		think; consider	(26)
·以来		since	(16)
议	(yì)	discuss; deliberate	(27)
饮	(yǐn)	喝	(21)
饮料		beverage; drink	(21)
饮食		food and drink; diet	(23)
·饮茶		喝茶	(21)
英	(yīng)	petal; Ying (*short for U.K.*)	(6)
英国		Britain	(6)
英国人		the British	(6)
英文		英语	(9)
英语		English (language)	(6)
应	(yīng)	should; ought to	(18)
应该		should; ought to	(18)
迎	(yíng)	meet; greet; welcome	(26)
迎接		receive; meet; greet	(26)
赢	(yíng)	win; gain profit	(28)
赢利		earn a profit	(28)
用	(yòng)	use; utilize; employ; apply	(13)
用功		work hard	(28)
优	(yōu)	good; excellent	(24)
优惠		preferential; favorable	(24)

	优先	have priority; take precedence; have precedence	(24)
由	(yóu)	by sb.; by means of	(29)
	由于	owing to; due to; as a result of	(29)
	由…做东	play the host by	(29)
有	(yǒu)	have; there be	(3)
	有本子	have notebook(s)	(3)
	有力	strong; powerful; vigorous	(28)
	有利	advantageous; beneficial; favorable	(28)
	有书	have book(s)	(3)
	·有的时候	sometimes	(3)
	·有名	be well-known; famous	(12)
	·有钱人	the rich; the wealthy	(24)
	·有心	have a mind to; intentionally; purposely	(23)
	·有心人	person who is resolved to do sth.useful; observant and conscientious person	(23)
友	(yǒu)	friend(s)	(13)
	友好	friendly; close friend(s)	(13)
	友情	friendly sentiments	
	友人	friend(s)	(13)
于	(yú)	to; in; on; at	(27)
鱼	(yú)	fish	(22)
语	(yǔ)	language; word; say; speak	(6)
	语言	language	(11)
预	(yù)	in advance; beforehand	(26)
	预先	in advance; beforehand	(26)
	预约	预先约好	(26)
元	(yuán)	unit of money	(24)
员	(yuán)	*a person engaged in some field of activity*	(21)
远	(yuǎn)	be far away (in time or space)	(8)
	远不远	be far away or not	(8)
	·远见	foresight	(8)
约	(yuē)	agree; make an appointment; arrange	(26)
	约好	make an appointment in advance	(26)
	约会	make an appointment; make an arrangement to meet	(26)
月	(yuè)	moon; month	(7)

Z

在	(zài)	be at (in,on) (a place) ; exist	(8)
	在不在	be in (a place) or not	(8)

在不在家		be at home or not	(8)
在家		be at home	(8)
在哪儿		where be	(8)
再	(zài)	again	(14)
再回去		go back again	(14)
再见		see you again	(14)
再来		come again	(14)
再去		go again	(14)
·再说		put off until some time later	(14)
·再三		over and over again; repeatedly	(14)
早	(zǎo)	early	
早安		早上好	(13)
早上		morning	(13)
早上好		good morning	(13)
·早饭		breakfast	(17)
·早日		at an early date	(13)
怎	(zěn)	why; how	(18)
怎么		why; how	(18)
怎么样		how; what; how are things; what do you think	(18)
怎么走		how to go	(19)
·怎样		怎么样	(18)
子	(zǐ)	*a particle–zi used to form a name zi-groups*	(2)
子女		son(s) and daughter(s)	(4)
字	(zì)	*zi* (Sinogram; Sinograph); script	(12)
总	(zǒng)	assemble; gather; general; total	(9)
总公司		head office of a corporation; head company	(9)
总经理		general or executive manager	(9)
·总理		premier; prime minister	(9)
·总是		always; at all time	(9)
走	(zǒu)	walk; go by walk; leave	(19)
·走路		walk; go on foot	(26)
昨	(zuó)	yesterday	(8)
昨天		yesterday	(8)
作	(zuò)	do	(9)
作业		school assignment	(9)
·作家		writer; author	(9)
·作用		function; action; effect	(13)
坐	(zuò)	sit	(13)
做	(zuò)	do	(7)
做成		accomplish; attain; achieve	(28)

做东		act as host to sb.	(24)
做什么		what to do	(7)
做主		decide; have the final say	(23)
最	(zuì)	most; least; best	(18)
最大		largest; greatest	(18)
最高		highest; tallest	(18)
最好		best; first-rate; had better; it would be best	(18)
最后		lastly; finally	(29)
最近		recently; the near future; nearest	(18)
最小		least; smallest	(18)

ZH

斩	(zhǎn)	chop; cut; kill	(22)
站	(zhàn)	stand; stop; station	(19)
长	(zhǎng)	chief; head	(27)
账	(zhàng)	account; account book	(24)
账单		bill; account; check	(24)
找	(zhǎo)	look for; hunt for; try to discover	(24)
找东西		look for sth.	(24)
找工作		look for a job	(24)
找钱		give change	(24)
找人		look for sb.	(24)
照	(zhào)	shine; light up	(29)
照顾		look after; care for	(29)
折	(zhé)	discount; rebate; discount	(24)
这	(zhè)	this	(11)
这儿	(zhèr)	here	(11)
这里	(zhèli)	这儿	(22)
这位		this man (woman) (*a polite form*)	(12)
·这样		like this	(18)
真	(zhēn)	true; real; really; indeed	(26)
真的		real; true	(26)
真快		really fast	(26)
真正		real; genuine; really	(26)
蒸	(zhēng)	steam	(22)
正	(zhèng)	just (doing sth.) ; upright; straight	(12)
正好		happen to	
正式		formal	(29)
正在		in process of; in the course of; be doing	(26)
只	(zhī)	*a measure-zi*	(22)

一只鸭		one duck	(22)
知	(zhī)	know; be aware (of)	(18)
知道		know; realize; be aware of	(18)
知识	(zhīshi)	knowledge; intellect	(18)
职	(zhí)	duty; job; position	(29)
职工		workers and staff members	(29)
·职业		occupation; profession; vocation	(29)
·职员		clerk; office worker; staff member	(29)
中	(zhōng)	middle; centre	(6)
中餐		Chinese cuisine; Chinese food	(24)
中国		China	(6)
中国人		Chinese (people)	(6)
中间		among; between; centre; middle	(18)
中文		the Chinese language and literature	(9)
中午		noon	(18)
·中饭		lunch	(17)
·中介		intermediary; medium	(12)
钟	(zhōng)	bell; clock	(19)
重	(zhòng)	be heavy; weighty; important	(28)
重视		attach importance to; think highly of; lay stress on	(28)
·重要		important; significant; essential; major	(28)
·重点		key point; emphasis; focus	(28)
周	(zhōu)	Zhou(*a surname*); week; circumference; circle	(26)
周到		thoughtful; considerate	(26)
主	(zhǔ)	host; owner; be in charge of; preside over	(23)
主人		host; master; owner	(23)
主食		staple food; principal food	(23)
·主体		main body; main or principal part	(23)
·主要		main; major; principal	(23)
祝	(zhù)	congratulate; celebrate	(11)
祝贺		congratulate; felicitate	(27)
祝寿		congratulate (an elderly person) on his or her birthday	(11)
专	(zhuān)	special	(9)
专门		special; specialized; concentrated	(9)
专业		special field of study	(9)
·专长		special skills; speciality	(9)
·专家		expert; specialist	(9)
·专有		related to a particular person or thing	(9)
·专有		related to a particular person or thing	

附录3 "唱读和口译"答案
Appendix 3 Key to Read aloud and interpret

第十六课

1. 还……没……(呢)　　　　　not... yet
   还没有来(呢)　　　　　　have not come yet
   还没有回来(呢)　　　　　have not come back yet
   还没有去(呢)　　　　　　have not gone yet
   还没有回去(呢)　　　　　have not gone back yet
   还没有看(呢)　　　　　　have not seen/read it yet
   还没有看见(呢)　　　　　have not seen it yet
2. 打　　　　　　　　　　　make (a phone call)
   打电话　　　　　　　　　make a phone call; talk on the phone
   打手机　　　　　　　　　make a phone call with a hand phone
3. 给　　　　　　　　　　　to (indicating the recipient)
   给他打电话　　　　　　　make a phone call to him
   给他办公室打电话　　　　make a phone call to him in his office
4. 号码　　　　　　　　　　number
   电话号码　　　　　　　　phone number
   手机号码　　　　　　　　hand phone number

第十七课

1. 向……问好　　　　　　　say hello to (sb.)
   向她问好　　　　　　　　say hello to her
   向老师问好　　　　　　　say hello to the teacher
   向大家问好　　　　　　　say hello to everybody
   向你父母问好　　　　　　say hello to your parents
2. 好　　　　　　　　　　　good (large in size, amount, etc.)
   好久　　　　　　　　　　a good long time
   好几天　　　　　　　　　a good number of days
   好长时间　　　　　　　　a good long time
   好几个人　　　　　　　　a good number of people

附录3 "唱读和口译"答案

3. 好久	a good long time
好久不见了	have not seen/met for a (good) long time
好久没来了	have not come for a (good) long time
好久没看见王同了	have not seen Wang Tong for a (good) time
好久没去过上海了	have not been to Shanghai for a (good) long time
4. 要	need; will (do sth.)
人人都要吃饭	Everybody need to eat.
白天要工作,晚上还要学习	will work at day and study in the evening
明天要去上海	will go to Shanghai tomorrow
星期天要去看王教授	will go and see Prof. Wang on Sunday
5. 麻烦	trouble; bother; troublesome
太麻烦	bother too much
麻烦您了	I have bothered you.
不敢麻烦您	I will not bother you.
6. 请你……	invite you...
请你吃饭	invite you to dinner
请你去上海	invite you to go to Shanghai
请你辅导汉语	invite you to help with Chinese
7. 不敢	dare not
不敢麻烦你	dare not bother you/I will not bother you
不敢见你	dare not see you/face you up
不敢给你打电话	dare not make a call to you
不敢请你吃饭	dare not invite you to dinner

第十八课

1. 饭	meal
早饭	breakfast
吃早饭	have breakfast
午饭(中饭)	lunch
吃午饭(吃中饭)	have lunch
晚饭	supper
吃晚饭	have supper
2. 应该	must; should
应该做	should do
这是我应该做的	This is what should do.
应该去北语学汉语	should go to BLCU to study Chinese
应该我请你	It should be me to treat you.
3. 点	o'clock; an iron tablet used in the ancient time to report the hours by knocking at it
几点	what time of o'clock?

	上午八点	eight in the morning
	中午十二点	twelve at noon
	晚上六点	six in the evening
4.	好像	seem; as if; it is like
	好像在长安街	It seems it is on Chang'an Street.
	好像要生病	as if one is about to be sick
	好像有你的电话	I think somebody called you on the phone.
	好像是马阳	I think it is Ma Yang.
5.	见	see; meet
	再见	Good-bye! See you again!
	晚上见	See you in the evening.
	下午见	See you in the afternoon.
	明天见	See you tomorrow.
	星期六见	See you on Saturday.

第十九课

1.	面	side; a suffix to words indicating the bearings
	东面	the east
	西面	the west
	南面	the south
	北面	the north
	上面	above; top
	下面	beneath; bottom
2.	从……向……	from... towards...
	从这儿向西	towards the west from here
	从天安门广场向南	towards the south from Tian'anmen Square
	从北京大学南门向东	towards the east from the southern gate of Peking University
	从南京向北	towards the north from Nanjing
3.	从……到……	from... to...
	从南京到北京	from Nanjing to Beijing
	从上海到西安	from Shanghai to Xi'an
	从韩国到日本	from Korea to Japan
	从中国到美国	from China to US
4.	什么时候?	What time? When?
	上午八点	eight in the morning
	下午四点	four in the afternoon
	晚上九点	nine in the evening
	两点十分	ten past two
	六点二十分	twenty past six

5. 多长时间？	How long (time)?
二十分钟	twenty minutes
一个小时	an hour
二十四个小时	twenty-four hours
两个小时四十分钟	two hours and forty minutes

第二十一课

1. 喝	drink
喝茶	drink/have tea
喝红茶	drink/have black tea
喝绿茶	drink/have green tea
喝龙井	drink/have the Longjing tea
喝咖啡	drink/have coffee
喝酒	drink any alcoholic drink
喝红酒	drink red wine
喝白酒	drink spirit
喝啤酒	drink beer
2. 喜欢	like; be fond of
喜欢林小姐	like Miss Lin
喜欢中国	like China
喜欢看书	like reading (books)
喜欢喝茶	like (drinking) tea
喜欢喝酒	like drinking (any alcoholic drink)
喜欢在饭店吃饭	like eating in a restaurant
3. 瓶	bottle
一瓶酒	a bottle of an alcoholic drink (wine, spirit, etc.)
两瓶红酒	two bottles of red wine
三瓶啤酒	three bottles of beer

第二十二课

1. 菜	vegetables; dish (amount of cooked vegetables, meat, etc.)
白菜	Chinese cabbage
青菜	green vegetable
热菜	hot dish
凉菜	cold dish
点菜	order a dish
吃菜	help oneself with a dish
2. 烧	burn; a way of cooking (stew after frying or fry after stewing)
烧鸡	braised chicken

烧鸭	braised duck
烧烤	barbecue
3. 红烧	braise with brown sauce
红烧肉	braised pork with brown sauce
红烧鱼	braised fish with brown sauce
红烧鲤鱼	braised carp with brown sauce
红烧豆腐	braised bean curd with brown sauce
4. 烤	roast
烤鱼	roast fish
烤肉	roast meat
烤鸭	roast duck
北京烤鸭	roast Peking duck
5. 清蒸	steam in clear soup
清蒸鸡	steamed chicken in clear soup
清蒸鱼	steamed fish in clear soup
清蒸鲤鱼	steamed carp in clear soup
6. 家常	homely; domestic trivia
家常菜	homely dish
家常饭	homely meal
家常豆腐	bean curd cooked with chili sauce
家常话	chitchat

第二十三课

1. 子 (zi)	*a nominal suffix*
包子	steamed round dumpling
儿子	son
饺子	boiled dumpling in the shape of half moon
里子	lining
面子	outer material
2. 吃吃	have a bite
说说	just talk/speak (about it)
想想	just think (about it)
叫叫	try to call out
看看	have a look
问问	just try to ask
3. 南方人	southerner
北方人	northerner
东方人	eastern (people)
西方人	western (people)

第二十四课

1. 共计	add up to
共计 52 人	fifty-two people all together
共计八百(800)元	eight hundred yuan in total
共计七百九十(790)元	seven hundred and ninety yuan in total
共计两千二百二十(2220)元	two thousand two hundred and twenty yuan in total
共计两千二百二十二(2222)元	two thousand two hundred and twenty-two yuan in total
共计四千五百一十六(4516)元	four thousand five hundred and sixteen yuan in total
共计三千零二十一元 (3021)	(零 líng: zero) three thousand and twenty-one yuan in total
2. 得	a structural particle to indicate the verbal complement of manner and potentiality
吃得太多	eat too much
吃得不少	have not eaten too little (have eaten quite a lot)
吃得很好	eat good food or satisfactorily
说得很好	talk well
说得不好	do not talk well
走得太快	walk too quickly
看得不快	do not read fast
买得不少	have not bought too little (have bought quite a lot)
3. 钱	money
有钱	have money; rich
没(有)钱	not have money; poor
给钱	give/pay money
钱很多	there is a lot of money
钱太少	there is too little money

第二十六课

1. 路	road
马路	road
公路	highway
大路	main road
小路	side walk
2. 过	pass; past
路过	pass by

	经过	pass; go through
	走过	pass; go by
	飞过	fly over
3.	正在	in the progress of
	正在开会	to be having a meeting
	正在会客	to be meeting with a guest
	正在吃饭	to be having a meal
	正在打电话	to be on the phone
	正在买东西	to be shopping
4.	您请……	Will you please... ?
	您请坐	Will you please have a seat?
	您请里面坐	Will you please come in (and have a seat) ?
	您请这儿坐	Will you please sit here?
	您请那儿坐	Will you please sit there?
	您请喝水	Will you please have some water?
	您请喝茶	Will you please have some tea?
	您请喝酒	Will you please have a drink (of wine) ?
	您请吃菜	Will you please help yourself with some dish?
5.	会	know (a skill or how to do sth.); likely; 一会儿 short while
	会说汉语	able to speak Chinese
	会写汉字	(写 xiě: write) can write characters
	开会	have a meeting
	会客	meet a guest
	会客室	reception room
	不会有人接电话	it is likely that no one will answer the phone
	最近不会去上海	one is not likely to go to Shanghai recently
	等一会儿	wait for a while
	一会儿就来	will come in no time

第二十七课

1.	刚	a short while ago; just
	刚来	just came
	刚回来	just came back
	刚从上海回来	just came back from Shanghai
	刚到	has just arrived
	刚到这里	has just arrived here
	刚走	just left
	刚散会	the meeting has just finished
	刚吃过午饭	have just finished lunch
	刚去过那里	have been there a short time ago

附录3 "唱读和口译"答案

2.	听说	It is said; I (or any one) heard
	听说王教授身体不太好	It is said that Prof. Wang is not well.
	听说林小姐要回韩国	I heard that Miss Lin was returning to Korea.
	听说林董事长要来中国	I heard that Lin the board director was coming to China
3.	关于	about; concerning
	关于合作的事	things about the cooperation
	关于合作项目	about the joint project
	关于软件设计	about the designing of soft wares
	关于生日晚会	about the birthday party
4.	件	*a measure zi used with 1) individual matters or things; 2) piece*
	软件	software
	一件事	a matter
	这件事	this matter

第二十八课

1.	希望	hope; wish
	希望早日见到你	hope to see you soon
	希望你们合作成功	hope your cooperation will be a success
	希望你常常来北京	hope you come to Beijing often
	希望大家都喜欢	hope you all like it
	有希望	have hope; hopeful
	有成功的希望	there is hope to succeed
	没希望	there is no hope; hopeless
	没成功的希望	there is no hope to succeed
2.	一定	sure; must
	一定来	sure to come
	一定很高兴	must be very happy
	一定能成功	will succeed for sure
	一定有希望	there must be hope
	不一定	not sure
	不一定能来	to be not sure to come
	不一定能成功	it is not certain that it will succeed
	不一定有希望	it is not certain that there is hope
3.	重视	attach importance to; think highly
	很重视	attach great importance to
	不重视	do not attach importance to; neglect
	很重视这件事	attach great importance to this matter
	很重视这个项目	attach great importance to this project
	很重视上海的合作项目	attach great importance to the joint project with Shanghai

第二十九课

1. 消息	message; news; information
有什么消息	Is there any news?
没有消息	There is not any news.
好消息	good news
有个好消息	There is a piece of good news.
刚听到的消息	news that one has just heard
晚来的消息	new that has come late
很关心马建的消息	concerned with information about Ma jian
2. 参加	take part in; participate in
参加工作	participate in the work; start to be employed
参加谈判	participate in the negotiation
参加生日晚会	attend the birthday party
3. 必须	must
必须参加	must take part in
必须成功	must succeed
必须去看王教授	must go and see Prof. Wang
必须由我做东	I must play host
4. 一起,和……一起	together; with
他们在一起	They stay together
我们一起去吧	Let's go together
他们一起在北京饭店吃饭	They have dinner together in Beijing Hotel
三木和林正美一起去给王教授祝寿了	Sanmu and Lin Zhengmei went together to congratulate Prof. Wang on his birthday.
林正美要和她父母一起回国	Lin Zhengmei is going back to her own country with her parents.
5. 正式	formal; official
正式职工	full-time worker
正式职业	full-time job
正式工作	full-time work
6. 就	1) indicating something that will happen in no time or has happened early; 2) exactly; precisely
早就认识了	have known (each other) long time ago
就来	come in no time
一会儿就来	come after a while
十分钟就到	come in ten minutes
车站就在那儿	The station/bus stop is right there.
以后就是正式职工了	become a full employee from now on
那就太好了	It is just fine in that case

附录3 "唱读和口译"答案

就叫我小周吧	Just call me Xiao Zhou.
就在沙发上坐吧	Sit in the sofa then.
7. 担心	worried about; anxious about
很担心	very anxious about
非常担心	extremely anxious about
担心您的身体	worried about your health
担心他的健康	worried about his health
担心她不回来	fear that she would not come back
8. 哪能	how can
哪能让您请我？	How can that be that you treat me?
哪能让您不高兴？	How can we make you disappointed?
我哪能走在您前面？	How can I go before you?
王教授岁数大了，哪能让他坐公共汽车？	How can we let Prof. Wang take the bus, as he is so old?
9. 死	1) die; 2) used as a complement of degree meaning extremely
死了	died
没死	not dead
不能死	can not die
不会死	impossible to die
高兴死了(非常高兴)	extremely happy
担心死了(非常担心)	extremely anxious
累死了(非常累)	extremely tired
10. 地	a structural particle indicating an adverbial
热情地关心	concerned about warmly
热情地欢迎	warmly welcome
高兴地说	gladly say

北大版对外汉语教材·短期培训系列·组合汉语

48小时汉语速成
基础篇

Learn Chinese in 48 Hours
—A Crash Course of Elementary Chinese

练习册
Exercise Book

下 册
Volume Two

编 著　吕必松
英文审订　鲁健骥
英文翻译　赵萍萍
　　　　　袁 媛

目 录

第十六课　马先生在家吗?	1
Lesson Sixteen　Is Mr. Ma at Home?	
第十七课　请你替我向她问好	4
Lesson Seventeen　Please Say Hello to Her	
第十八课　我想请你吃午饭	7
Lesson Eighteen　I Would Like to Invite You to Lunch	
第十九课　北京饭店在哪儿?	10
Lesson Nineteen　Where is Beijing Hotel?	
第二十课　复习(四)	13
Lesson Twenty　Review (4)	
第二十一课　你们喝什么饮料?	16
Lesson Twenty-one　What Kind of Drinks Would You Like?	
第二十二课　你们想吃什么菜?	20
Lesson Twenty-two　What Kind of Dish Would You Like?	
第二十三课　你们要什么主食?	23
Lesson Twenty-three　What Staple Food Would You Like?	
第二十四课　共计九百零二元	26
Lesson Twenty-four　Altogether 902 Yuan	
第二十五课　复习(五)	30
Lesson Twenty-five　Review (5)	

第二十六课　马总正在开会 ……………………………………………………… 33
Lesson Twenty-six　General Manager Ma is at a Meeting

第二十七课　让您久等了 …………………………………………………………… 37
Lesson Twenty-seven　Sorry for Having Kept You Waiting So Long

第二十八课　这是互利双赢的好项目 …………………………………………… 40
Lesson Twenty-eight　This is a Mutually Beneficial Win-win Project

第二十九课　贵客到了 ……………………………………………………………… 43
Lesson Twenty-nine　The Distinguished Guest is Arriving

第三十课　复习(六) ………………………………………………………………… 46
Lesson Thirty　Review(6)

附录　练习题答案 …………………………………………………………………… 49
Appendix　Key to the Exercises

第十六课　马先生在家吗？
Lesson Sixteen　Is Mr. Ma at Home?

一、复习并记住下列部件的名称 Review the names of the following *Hanzi* components and learn them by heart

扌(打)　纟(给)　辶(还)　文(这)

二、把下列各组汉字中相同的部件写在括号里 Write the common component of each group of *Hanzi* in the bracket

1. 打　接　授　（　）
2. 给　经　绍　（　）
3. 吗　码　（　）

三、说出下列部件的名称 Tell the names of the following *Hanzi* components

几(机)　人(认)　建(健)　生(姓)　你(您)

四、把下列汉字的义符写在括号里 Write the meaning components of the following *Hanzi* in the brackets

海（　）说（　）打（　）授（　）想（　）他（　）她（　）
吗（　）叫（　）远（　）林（　）机（　）

五、完成下面的句子 Complete the following sentences

1. 马先生在_____？
2. 马先生不_____家。
3. 您可以_____他办公室打电话。
4. 您可以打他办公室的_____。

5. 您_____他的手机吧。
6. 我没有他公司_____电话号码。
7. 他的手机_____是幺三零五二四六六七八八。

六、把字词连成句子 Make a sentence with each group of zi and zi-groups

1. 呢 没 还 回 马先生 家
2. 吗 三木先生 韩国 去 回 了
3. 您 打 的 他 吧 电话 办公室
4. 打 您 的 他 吧 手机
5. 他 没 手机 接 的 人

七、翻译下面的词语和句子 Translate the following zi-groups and sentences

1. 汉译英 Chinese to English

   (1) 韩国公司

   (2) 电话号码

   (2) 手机号码

   (3) 打他的手机

   (4) 打他办公室的电话

   (5) 公司的电话号码

2. 英译汉 English to Chinese

   (1) He went to an American company.

   (2) You'd better phone his company's telephone.

   (3) You can call his mobile phone.

   (4) I don't have his mobile phone number.

八、阅读理解 Reading comprehension

三木给马家打电话

三木给马先生家打电话。是马太太接的电话。

三木问马太太:"马先生在家吗?"

第十六课 马先生在家吗?

　　马太太说:"马先生在公司,还没有回家呢。"她叫三木给马先生的办公室打电话。

　　三木说,他给马先生的办公室打过电话了,办公室的电话没人接。马太太叫三木打马先生的手机。马先生的手机号码是13302466788。

九、根据阅读内容选择正确答案,在正确答案后面的方框内打√
Tick the right answer in each group according to what you read above

1. 谁给马先生家打电话了?
　(1) 王老师给马先生家打电话了。　□
　(2) 王太太给马先生家打电话了。　□
　(3) 三木先生给马先生家打电话了。　□
　(4) 林正美给马先生家打电话了。　□

2. 三木打给马先生的电话是谁接的?
　(1) 三木打给马先生的电话是马太太接的。　□
　(2) 三木打给马先生的电话是马先生的儿子接的。　□
　(3) 三木打给马先生的电话是马先生的女儿接的。　□
　(4) 三木打给马先生的电话是马先生接的。　□

第十七课　请你替我向她问好
Lesson Seventeen　Please Say Hello to Her

一、复习并记住下列部件的名称 Review the names of the following *Hanzi* components and learn them by heart

火(烦)　车(辅)　饣(饭)

二、把下列各组汉字中相同的部件写在括号里 Write the common component of each group of *Hanzi* in the bracket

1. 忙　快　（　）
2. 麻　康　（　）
3. 教　做　敢　（　）

三、说出下列部件的名称 Tell the names of the following *Hanzi* components

口(问　向)　林(麻)　广(麻　康)　辶(过　远)

四、把下列汉字的音符写在括号里 Write the sound components of the following *Hanzi* in the brackets

1. 吗（　）
2. 码（　）
3. 们（　）
4. 问（　）
5. 字（　）
6. 机（　）
7. 认（　）
8. 什（　）
9. 您（　）

4

第十七课　请你替我向她问好

五、完成下面的句子 Complete the following sentences

1. 请你_____我_____王教授问好。
2. 白天工作很_____，_____上还_____学习。
3. 你是个_____忙人，我不_____麻烦你。
4. 我妈妈要_____你打电话，她想_____你吃饭。

六、把字词连成句子 Make a sentence with each group of zi and zi-groups

1. 不 了 见 好 久
2. 工作 吗 忙 你
3. 白天 不 工作 忙，很 工作 晚上 忙
4. 不 他 敢 你 麻烦
5. 要 马太太 林小姐 打 给 电话
6. 请 马太太 要 林小姐 午饭 吃

七、阅读理解 Reading comprehension

马建给林小姐打电话

马建在韩国学习过，和林正美早就认识了。他们是在韩国认识的，林正美给他辅导过韩语。马建好久没见到林正美了，很想见到她。他今天给林正美打电话，问她工作忙不忙。林正美说，她很忙，白天要工作，晚上还要学习汉语。马建想给她辅导，林正美说他是个大忙人，她不敢麻烦他。马建告诉(gàosu:tell)林正美，他母亲想请她吃饭，要给她打电话。林正美听(tīng:hear)了很高兴，说："太好了！谢谢她，请替我向她问好。"

八、根据阅读内容选择正确答案，在正确答案后面的方框内打√ Tick the right answer in each group according to what you read above

1. 马建和林正美是在哪儿认识的？
   (1) 他们是在中国认识的。　☐
   (2) 他们是在日本认识的。　☐

5

(3) 他们是在美国认识的。
(4) 他们是在韩国认识的。

2. 马建在哪儿学习过?
   (1) 马建在英国学习过。
   (2) 马建在美国学习过。
   (3) 马建在韩国学习过。
   (4) 马建在日本学习过。

3. 马建给林正美打电话说什么了?
   (1) 他很想她。
   (2) 他想见她。
   (3) 他想给林正美辅导汉语。
   (4) 他妈妈想请林正美吃饭。

4. 听说(tīngshuō:It is said)马建的妈妈要请她吃饭,林正美同意(tóngyì: agree)了吗?
   (1) 她同意了。
   (2) 她没同意。

第十八课　我想请你吃午饭
Lesson Eighteen　I Would Like to Invite You to Lunch

一、复习并记住下列部件的名称 Review the names of the following *Hanzi* components and learn them by heart

矢(知)　灬(点)　丰(用)　冂(用)

二、把下列各组汉字中相同的部件写在括号里 Write the common component of each group of *Hanzi* in the bracket

1. 较　辅　（　）
2. 点　店　（　）
3. 间　问　们　（　）
4. 怎　作　昨　（　）

三、说出下列部件的名称 Tell the names of the following *Hanzi* components

丷(关)　天(关)　小(系)　心(怎)　匕(比)

四、把下列汉字的义符写在括号里 Write the meaning components of the following *Hanzi* in the brackets

1. 吃（　）
2. 饭（　）
3. 店（　）
4. 点（　）

五、完成下面的句子 Complete the following sentences

1. 我_____我先生想请你_____三木先生吃午饭。

2. 星期六中_____十二_____。
3. 在_____？
4. _____北京饭店。
5. 你知道北京饭店_____哪儿吗？
6. 我可以_____人。

六、把字词连成句子 Make a sentence with each group of *zi* and *zi*-groups

1. 你 吗 忙 最近
2. 最近 吗 好 身体 马太太
3. 你 北京饭店 哪儿 在 知道 吗
4. 十二点 中午 星期六
5. 见 星期六

七、翻译下面的词语和句子 Translate the following *zi*-groups and sentences

1. 汉译英 Chinese to English
    (1) 儿子和女儿
    (2) 王明英和马飞
    (3) 北京饭店很大。
    (4) 今天中午我们请你吃午饭。
    (5) 马总八点来公司。

2. 英译汉 English to Chinese
    (1) Japan and America.
    (2) What time do you have lunch?
    (3) Mrs. Ma invited us to lunch yesterday.
    (4) It's very nice!

八、阅读理解 Reading comprehension

马太太请林小姐吃午饭

马太太叫王明英。她给林正美小姐打电话,请她吃午饭。林正美小姐很高兴,说:"太好了!"她问:什么时候?在哪儿?王明英告诉(gàosu:tell)她:吃饭的时间是星期六中午十二点,地点(dìdiǎn: place)在北京饭店,她还请了三木先生,马先生也去。王明英问林小姐,她知不知道北京饭店在哪儿,林小姐说她可以问人。

九、根据阅读内容选择正确答案,在正确答案后面的方框内打√
Tick the right answer in each group according to what you read above

1. 王明英请谁吃饭?
   (1) 王明英请马飞的老师吃饭。☐
   (2) 王明英请王教授吃饭。☐
   (3) 王明英请王同吃饭。☐
   (4) 王明英请三木和林正美吃饭。☐

2. 王明英请他们在哪儿吃饭?
   (1) 王明英请他们在家吃饭。☐
   (2) 王明英请他们在公司吃饭。☐
   (3) 王明英请他们在北京饭店吃饭。☐
   (4) 王明英请他们在办公室吃饭。☐

3. 他们什么时候在北京饭店吃饭?
   (1) 星期五中午十二点。☐
   (2) 星期六中午十二点。☐
   (3) 星期日中午十二点。☐
   (4) 星期二中午十二点。☐

4. 北京饭店在哪儿?
   (1) 北京饭店在天安门广场。☐
   (2) 北京饭店在北京大学。☐
   (3) 北京饭店在北京语言大学。☐
   (4) 北京饭店在长安街。☐

5. 林小姐知道北京饭店在哪儿吗?
   (1) 她知道。☐
   (2) 她不知道。☐

第十九课　北京饭店在哪儿？
Lesson Nineteen　Where is Beijing Hotel?

一、复习并记住下列部件的名称 Review the names of the following *Hanzi* components, and learn them by heart

钅(钟)　立(站)　辶(走)

二、把下列各组汉字中相同的部件写在括号里 Write the common component of each group of *Hanzi* in the bracket

1. 分　公　（　）
2. 南　幸　（　）
3. 多　名　（　）
4. 钟　贵　（　）
5. 应　兴　（　）
6. 那　哪　都　（　）
7. 最　星　是　白　（　）

三、说出下列部件的名称 Tell the names of the following *Hanzi* components

八（分）　八（共）　十（南）　十（早）　二（离）　西（要）
气（汽）　免（晚）　中（钟）　不（还）　口（可）

四、把下列汉字的义符写在括号里 Write the meaning components of the following *Hanzi* in the brackets

1. 汽（　）
2. 钟（　）
3. 站（　）
4. 烦（　）

5. 辅（ ）
6. 问（ ）

五、完成下面的句子 Complete the following sentences

1. ＿＿＿＿＿,北京饭店在哪儿?
2. 去北京饭店＿＿＿＿＿走?
3. 您可以从这儿＿＿＿＿＿西。
4. 北京饭店＿＿＿＿＿这儿远不远?
5. 要是坐公共汽车,＿＿＿＿＿时间能到?
6. 打的比较快,十分＿＿＿＿＿就到。

六、把字词连成句子 Make a sentence with each group of zi and zi-groups

1. 哪儿　在　天安门
2. 在　北京语言大学　东面　北京大学
3. 远　这儿　天安门广场　离　不
4. 就　南面　在　车站
5. 这儿　去　从　北京大学,就　十分钟　到　打的

七、阅读理解 Reading comprehension

问路(wèn lù: ask the way)

　　林正美小姐在去北京饭店的路(lù:road; way)上。王明英请她去北京饭店吃午饭,她不知道去北京饭店怎么走。她问一位小姐北京饭店在哪儿。那位小姐说,她也不知道北京饭店在哪儿,好像在南面。林正美又(yòu:again)问一位先生去北京饭店怎么走。那位先生告诉(gàosu:tell)她:"北京饭店在天安门广场东面,您可以从这儿向西。"林正美又问:北京饭店离这儿远不远?多长时间能到?那位先生说:"北京饭店离这儿不太远,你可以坐公共汽车去,也可以打的去;坐公共汽车二十分钟能到,打的比较快,十分钟就到。"

八、根据阅读内容选择正确答案,在正确答案后面的方框内打√
Tick the right answer in each group according to what you read above

1. 林正美在去哪儿的路上问路？
   (1) 林正美在去北京大学的路上问路。☐
   (2) 林正美在去北京饭店的路上问路。☐

2. 林正美问路问了几个人？
   (1) 林正美问路问了两个人。☐
   (2) 林正美问路问了三个人。☐

3. 北京饭店离问路的地方(dìfang:place)远不远？
   (1) 北京饭店离问路的地方非常远。☐
   (2) 北京饭店离问路的地方不太远。☐

4. 从问路的地方去北京饭店,坐公共汽车多长时间能到？
   (1) 坐公共汽车二十分钟能到。☐
   (2) 坐公共汽车十分钟能到。☐

5. 从问路的地方去北京饭店,打的多长时间能到？
   (1) 打的十分钟能到。☐
   (2) 打的二十分钟能到。☐

第二十课 复习(四)
Lesson Twenty Review (4)

一、说出下列部件的名称 Tell the names of the following *Hanzi* components

1. 耂(老)　ナ(有)　严(看)　亠(离)　宀(实)　丷(关)
2. 亻(你)　讠(话)　女(姓)　氵(汉)　忄(快)　木(机)
   火(烦)　车(辅)　饣(饭)　扌(打)　纟(给)　钅(钟)
   立(站)　矢(知)
3. 刂(到)　匕(比)　建(健)　生(姓)
4. 亲(亲)　厶(去)　ㄗ(走)　灬(点)　匕(老)　大(奖)
   心(想)　生(星)
5. 辶(还)　冂(用)
6. 耒(用)　文(这)

二、阅读理解 Reading comprehension

朋友之间(zhījiān: between)

　　三木和马飞早就认识了,他们是老朋友,常常打电话互相(hùxiāng: each other)问好。一天,马飞给三木打电话,这次(cì: of times)是要请三木吃饭。三木没接到马飞的电话,就给马飞回电话。马飞办公室的电话也没人接,三木就打到马飞家里(lǐ: in, at)。马飞家里的电话是马太太接的,她说:"马先生还没回来呢,他办公室的电话没人接,你就打他的手机吧。"她说了马飞的手机号码。

　　马飞的儿子马建和林正美也是好朋友。他们是在韩国认识的。马建在韩国学习过,林正美给他辅导过韩语。他常常想林正美,想她的时候,就打电话问她工作忙不忙,身体好不好。就在马飞和三木互相打电话的那天,马建也给林正美打了电话。他在电话里说,他妈妈想请她吃饭,要给她打电话。林正美听(tīng: hear)

了非常高兴。她想,马太太请她吃饭,她就能见到马建了。

　　林正美接到了马太太的电话。马太太在电话里说,她和她先生想请她和三木先生在北京饭店吃午饭,时间是星期六中午十二点。

　　林小姐在去北京饭店的路(lù:way; road)上。她没去过北京饭店,不知道怎么走,就问路上的人。她问:"北京饭店在哪儿?怎么走?多长时间能到?"路上的人说:北京饭店在天安门广场东面,离这儿不太远,可以坐公共汽车去,也可以打的去。坐公共汽车二十分钟能到,打的比较快,十分钟就到。

三、根据阅读内容选择正确答案,在正确答案后面的方框内打√
Tick the right answer in each group according to what you read above

1. 马飞和三木常常他们互相打电话,是因为(yīnwèi:because)他们是老朋友。☐
   马飞和三木常常他们互相打电话,是因为要互相问好。☐
   马飞和三木常常他们互相打电话,是因为要互相请吃饭。☐

2. 三木给马飞家打电话,是因为他不知道马飞办公室的电话号码。☐
   三木给马飞家打电话,是因为马飞办公室的电话没人接。☐
   三木给马飞家打电话,是因为他要向马太太问好。☐

3. 马建给林正美打电话,是为了(wèile:for the sake of)问三木的手机号码。☐
   马建给林正美打电话,是为了向林正美问好。☐
   马建给林正美打电话,是为了告诉(gàosu:tell)她,他妈妈要请她吃饭。☐

4. 林正美很喜欢(xǐhuan:like)马建。☐
   林正美不喜欢马建。☐

5. 王明英和马飞请林正美和三木吃晚饭。☐
   王明英和马飞请林正美和三木吃早饭。☐
   王明英和马飞请林正美和三木吃午饭。☐

第二十课 复习(四)

6. 他们吃午饭的时间是星期六上午十一点。 ☐
   他们吃午饭的时间是星期天下午两点。 ☐
   他们吃午饭的时间是星期六中午十二点。 ☐

四、写一篇短文说说你和你的好朋友互相打电话的情况 Write an essay about a telephone conversation between your good friends and you

第二十一课 你们喝什么饮料？
Lesson Twenty-one What Kind of Drinks Would You Like?

一、复习并记住下列部件的名称 Review the names of the following *Hanzi* components, and learn them by heart

艹(茶) 米(料) 欠(欢) 酉(酒) 采(菜)

二、把下列各组汉字中相同的部件写在括号里 Write the common component of each group of *Hanzi* in the bracket

1. 菜 茶 英 （　）
2. 红 绿 给 （　）
3. 饮 饭 （　）
4. 饮 欢 （　）
5. 茶 亲 （　）
6. 务 办 （　）

三、说出下列部件的名称 Tell the names of the following *Hanzi* components

纟(绿) 饣(饮) 工(红) 非(啡) 欠(饮)

四、把下列汉字的义符写在括号里 Write the meaning components of the following *Hanzi* in the brackets

酒（　） 茶（　） 菜（　） 料（　） 喝（　） 欢（　）

五、把下列各组词语中读音相同的汉字写在括号里 Write the homophonic *Hanzi* in each *zi*-group in the bracket

1. 马飞 号码（　，　）

第二十一课　你们喝什么饮料？

2. 中国　分钟（　，　）
3. 星期　七天（　，　）
4. 十九　白酒（　，　）
5. 十个　时候（　，　）
6. 在家　再见（　，　）
7. 不是　办公室（　，　）

六、完成下面的句子 Complete the following sentences

1. 你们喝_____饮料？
2. 您喝茶_____喝咖啡？
3. 你们喜欢红茶_____绿茶？
4. 马太太喜欢喝绿_____。
5. 来两_____啤酒。

七、翻译下面的词语和句子 Translate the following zi-groups and sentences

1. 汉译英 Chinese to English
   (1) 好(hǎo)吃
   (2) 吃饭
   (3) 喝酒
   (4) 龙井茶很有名。
   (5) 林小姐喜欢吃中国菜。
   (6) 马太太不喜欢喝红茶。

2. 英译汉 English to Chinese
   (1) Would you like to drink beer?
   (2) What kind of drink would you like?
   (3) Would you like to drink tea or coffee?
   (4) Is Longjing tea black tea or green tea?
   (5) Does Mr. Ma like to drink black tea or green tea?

八、阅读理解 Reading comprehension

马太太问大家喝什么饮料

　　点菜的时候,马太太问大家喝什么饮料,马先生问林小姐喝茶还是喝咖啡。茶和咖啡都(dōu:all)是饮料。林小姐说,她喝茶。服务员说,有红茶,也有绿茶,她问林小姐喝红茶还是喝绿茶。马建知道林小姐喜欢喝什么茶。他说,林小姐喜欢喝龙井。龙井茶是绿茶。马太太说,正好她也喜欢喝龙井。马太太问三木喝什么,三木说他喝啤酒。马先生说他也喝啤酒。啤酒也是饮料。马太太问大家喝不喝酒,三木说,下午要工作,中午不能喝酒。马建知道林小姐喜欢喝红酒,就说:再来一瓶红酒吧,我妈妈和林小姐都能喝红酒。他希望(xīwàng:wish)林小姐高兴。

九、根据阅读内容选择正确答案,在正确答案后面的方框内打√ Tick the right answer in each group according to what you read above

1. 林小姐和马太太喝什么饮料?
　(1)林小姐喝茶,马太太喝咖啡。☐
　(2)林小姐喝咖啡,马太太喝茶。☐
　(3)林小姐和马太太都喝咖啡。☐
　(4)林小姐和马太太都喝茶。☐

2. 林小姐和马太太喜欢喝什么茶?
　(1)林小姐喜欢喝红茶,马太太喜欢喝绿茶。☐
　(2)林小姐喜欢喝绿茶,马太太喜欢喝红茶。☐
　(3)林小姐和马太太都喜欢喝绿茶。☐
　(4)林小姐和马太太都喜欢喝红茶。☐

3. 三木和马先生喝什么饮料?
　(1)三木喝啤酒,马先生喝咖啡。☐
　(2)三木喝咖啡,马先生喝啤酒。☐
　(3)三木和马先生都喝咖啡。☐
　(4)三木和马先生都喝啤酒。☐

第二十一课　你们喝什么饮料？

4. 马太太和林小姐喝酒了吗？
  (1) 她们没喝酒。 ☐
  (2) 她们喝白酒了。 ☐
  (3) 她们喝红酒了。 ☐
  (4) 她们喝白酒和红酒了。 ☐

第二十二课　你们想吃什么菜?
Lesson Twenty-two What Kind of Dish Would You Like?

一、复习并记住下列部件的名称 Review the names of the following *Hanzi* components, and learn them by heart

西(要)　冫(凉)　鸟(鸭)　斤(斩)

二、把下列各组汉字中相同的部件写在括号里 Write the common component of each group of *Hanzi* in the bracket

1. 鸡　欢　(　)
2. 鸭　鸡　(　)
3. 斩　近　(　)
4. 清　请　(　)
5. 鲤　理　(　)
6. 凉　习　(　)
7. 斩　较　(　)
8. 饺　较　(　)
9. 蒸　点　热　(　)
10. 烧　烤　烦　(　)

三、说出下列部件的名称 Tell the names of the following *Hanzi* components

氵(清)　鱼(鲤)　鸟(鸡)　多(够)　灬(蒸)　木(条)　广(腐)

四、把下列汉字的义符写在括号里 Write the meaning components of the following *Hanzi* in the brackets

鸡(　)　烤(　)　鲤(　)　清(　)　凉(　)　蒸(　)

第二十二课 你们想吃什么菜?

五、完成下面的句子 Complete the following sentences

1. 这是菜单,请你_____菜。
2. 林小姐_____客气了。
3. 你们喜欢吃_____菜?
4. 这里_____烤鸭很好。
5. 要一_____烤鸭。
6. 再要一_____红烧鲤鱼。

六、翻译下面的句子 Translate the following sentences

1. 汉译英 Chinese to English
   (1) 请林小姐点菜。
   (2) 您太客气了!
   (3) 你们喜欢喝什么茶?
   (4) 这里的烤鸭很好吃。

2. 英译汉 English to Chinese
   (1) Too many dishes.
   (2) I would like to have fish in brown sauce.
   (3) They like eating roast duck.
   (4) I don't like the plain boiled chicken here.

七、阅读理解 Reading comprehension

点菜

点过饮料以后(yǐhòu:after),马太太叫林小姐点菜。林小姐说她不会点。马太太叫三木点,三木叫马太太和马先生点。马太太问大家喜欢吃什么,马飞说,三木喜欢吃烤鸭,这里的烤鸭很好。三木说林小姐也喜欢吃烤鸭,她还喜欢吃鱼。马太太对(duì:to)服务员说:"要一只烤鸭,一条鲤鱼。"服务员说鲤鱼有清蒸的,也有红烧的,问他们要清蒸的还是要红烧的。马先生说红烧的好。马先生还想吃红烧肉和家常豆腐。马建提议(tíyì:suggest)点几个凉菜。他说,这里的白斩鸡很好,林小姐最喜欢吃白斩鸡。他们最后(zuìhòu:lastly)决定(juédìng:decide)要一只烤鸭,一条烧鲤鱼,一个红烧肉,一个家常豆腐,一个青菜和一个白斩鸡。

八、根据阅读内容选择正确答案，在正确答案后面的方框内打√
Tick the right answer in each group according to what you read above

1. 林小姐喜欢吃什么？
   (1) 林小姐喜欢吃烤鸭，不喜欢吃鱼。☐
   (2) 林小姐不喜欢吃烤鸭，喜欢吃鱼。☐
   (3) 林小姐不喜欢吃烤鸭，也不喜欢吃鱼。☐
   (4) 林小姐喜欢吃烤鸭，也喜欢吃鱼。☐

2. 三木喜欢吃什么？
   (1) 三木喜欢吃烤鸭，不喜欢吃红烧肉。☐
   (2) 三木喜欢吃烤鸭，不喜欢吃家常豆腐。☐
   (3) 三木喜欢吃家常豆腐，不喜欢吃烤鸭。☐
   (4) 三木喜欢吃烤鸭、红烧肉和家常豆腐。☐

3. 他们点了什么菜？
   (1) 他们点了烤鸭、红烧鲤鱼和青菜，没点红烧肉和白斩鸡。☐
   (2) 他们点了烤鸭、家常豆腐和白斩鸡，没点青菜和红烧鲤鱼。☐
   (3) 他们点了青菜和清蒸鲤鱼，没点红烧肉和白斩鸡。☐
   (4) 他们点了烤鸭、红烧鲤鱼、红烧肉、白斩鸡、青菜和家常豆腐。☐

4. 他们点了几只烤鸭、几条鲤鱼、几个青菜？
   (1) 他们点了一只烤鸭、两条鲤鱼、三个青菜。☐
   (2) 他们点了两只烤鸭、三条鲤鱼、一个青菜。☐
   (3) 他们点了三只烤鸭、两条鲤鱼、四个青菜。☐
   (4) 他们点了一只烤鸭、一条鲤鱼、一个青菜。☐

第二十三课 你们要什么主食?
Lesson Twenty-three What Staple Food Would You Like?

一、复习并记住下列部件的名称 Review the names of the following *Hanzi* components, and learn them by heart

⺌(尝)　王(现)　力(方)　勹(包)

二、把下列各组汉字中相同的部件写在括号里 Write the common component of each group of *Hanzi* in the bracket

1. 尝　常　(　)
2. 碗　码　(　)
3. 现　理　(　)
4. 尝　会　(　)
5. 饺　较　(　)
6. 前　豆　喜　(　)

三、说出下列部件的名称 Tell the names of the following *Hanzi* components

一(方)　王(理)　米(料)　见(现)　包(饱)　里(理)　友(爱)　玉(国)

四、把下列汉字的音符写在括号里 Write the sound components of the following *Hanzi* in the brackets

啡(　)　清(　)　鲤(　)　饱(　)　近(　)　现(　)　红(　)

五、完成下面的句子 Complete the following sentences

1. 我已经_____饱了。

2. 我＿＿＿＿见过王先生了。

3. 他们已经去＿＿＿＿马先生的公司了。

4. 我好久没吃面条＿＿＿＿。

5. 我以前不喜欢吃面食,现在也喜欢＿＿＿＿。

6. 面条、包子、饺子我＿＿＿＿爱吃。

7. 要不＿＿＿＿叫点心?

8. 再要一＿＿＿＿米饭,一＿＿＿＿面条。

六、翻译下面的词语和句子 Translate the following zi-groups and sentences

1. 汉译英 Chinese to English

(1) 去过。

(2) 看见了。

(3) 他没吃过烤鸭。

(4) 三木吃饱了,林小姐没吃饱。

2. 英译汉 English to Chinese

(1) Please have a taste (of sth.).

(2) Shall we order roast duck?

(3) Southerners like eating rice.

(4) There are enough dishes.

七、阅读理解 Reading comprehension

马太太问大家要什么主食

马太太问大家要什么主食,林小姐说她已经吃饱了,不吃主食了。马先生知道三木喜欢吃饺子,就点了一斤。马太太说北京饭店的饺子很好,叫林小姐也尝尝。马太太是南方人,以前只(zhǐ: only)爱吃米饭,现在也爱吃面食了。饺子、包子、面条她都爱吃。饺子、包子是用面做的,属于(shǔyú: belong to)面食。中国多数南方人喜欢吃米饭,多数北方人喜欢吃面食。米饭和面食都属于主食。马先生问大家要不要叫点心,三木说,都已经吃饱了,不要叫点心了。他们只吃了米饭、饺子和面条,没有叫点心。

第二十三课　你们要什么主食？

八、根据阅读内容选择正确答案，在正确答案后面的方框内打√
Tick the right answer in each group according to what you read above

1. 马太太叫林小姐尝尝什么？
   (1) 马太太叫林小姐尝尝米饭。☐
   (2) 马太太叫林小姐尝尝点心。☐
   (3) 马太太叫林小姐尝尝饺子。☐
   (4) 马太太叫林小姐尝尝烤鸭。☐

2. 马太太喜欢吃什么主食？
   (1) 马太太喜欢吃饺子，不喜欢吃米饭。☐
   (2) 马太太喜欢吃米饭，不喜欢吃饺子。☐
   (3) 马太太喜欢吃面条，也喜欢吃饺子。☐
   (4) 米饭、饺子、包子和面条她都喜欢吃。☐

3. 他们点了什么主食？
   (1) 他们点了米饭、饺子、包子和面条。☐
   (2) 他们点了米饭，没点饺子、包子和面条。☐
   (3) 他们点了饺子和面条，没点包子和米饭。☐
   (4) 他们点了米饭、饺子和面条，没点包子。☐

4. 林小姐和三木吃饱了吗？
   (1) 林小姐吃饱了，三木没吃饱。☐
   (2) 林小姐没吃饱，三木吃饱了。☐
   (3) 林小姐和三木都没吃饱。☐
   (4) 林小姐和三木都吃饱了。☑

第二十四课　共计九百零二元
Lesson Twenty-four　Altogether 902 Yuan

一、复习并记住下列部件的名称 Review the names of the following *Hanzi* components, and learn them by heart

彳(得)　戈(找)　尤(优)　戋(钱)　攵(做)

二、把下列各组汉字中括号里 Write the common component of each group of *Hanzi* in the bracket

1. 得　很　街　（　）
2. 买　实　（　）
3. 宜　姐　（　）
4. 南　计　早　千　（　）
5. 找　打　折　接　授　（　）

三、说出下列部件的名称 Tell the names of the following *Hanzi* components

钅(钱)　扌(找)　冫(凉)　尤(就)　攵(教)
斤(折)　欠(次)　食(餐)　元(远)

四、把下列汉字的义符写在括号里 Write the meaning components of the following *Hanzi* in the brackets

餐（　）　找（　）　折（　）　钱（　）　账（　）

五、把下列各组词语中读音相同的汉字写在括号里 Write the homophonic *Hanzi* in each group of *zi*-group in the bracket

1. 工人　公司（　,　）

2. 工作　请坐（　，　）

3. 北京　已经（　，　）

4. 前天　多少钱（　，　）

5. 一百元　服务员（　，　）

6. 小时　主食　五十（　，　，　）

7. 好久　十九　白酒（　，　，　）

六、完成下面的句子 Complete the following sentences

1. 林小姐吃_____很少

2. 我吃_____了。

3. 共计三百五十_____。

4. 打过八五_____了。

5. 这是我妈给我_____钱。

6. 我妈的钱_____我多。

7. 中餐很便_____。

8. 下回请你们_____西餐。

七、翻译下面的词语和句子 Translate the following zi-groups and sentences

1. 汉译英 Chinese to English

   (1) 不便宜

   (2) 你吃好了吗?

   (3) 一共二十五元。

   (4) 一共多少钱?

   (5) 这个菜很贵。

2. 英译汉 English to Chinese

   (1) Too expensive!

   (2) Can I have a discount?

   (3) 15% discount.

   (4) He does not like eating Western food.

   (5) Is twenty yuan enough?

八、阅读理解 Reading comprehension

结账

在饭店付(fù:pay)吃饭的钱叫结账,也叫买单、埋单(máidān: pay a bill)。结账的时候,马建问服务员多少钱。服务员给他账单,说:"共计902元。"他们常常到这儿吃饭,所以(suǒyǐ:so)有八折优惠。八折优惠也叫打八折。服务员告诉(gàosu:tell)他,已经打过八折了。马建给了服务员一千元,服务员找给他98元。林小姐说:"谢谢买单的"。因为(yīnwèi:because)是马建买的单,所以说"谢谢买单的"就是说"谢谢马建"。请人在饭店吃饭,请客的人付吃饭的钱。马建要说明这次是他妈妈请客,所以说:"这是我妈妈给我的钱。"意思(yìsi:meaning)是:他买单是替他妈妈买的。他还说,他妈妈的钱比他多。

大家都知道,西餐比较贵,中餐比西餐便宜。马太太说,下次请大家吃西餐。意思是:她有钱。三木说,下回他做东。

九、根据阅读内容选择正确答案,在正确答案后面的方框内打√ Tick the right answer in each group according to what you read above

1. 这次吃饭谁做东?
   (1) 这次吃饭王明英做东。 □
   (2) 这次吃饭马飞做东。 □
   (3) 这次吃饭马建做东。 □
   (4) 这次吃饭林正美做东。 □

2. 这次吃饭有优惠吗?
   (1) 这次吃饭没有优惠。 □
   (2) 这次吃饭有九折优惠。 □
   (3) 这次吃饭打了八五折。 □
   (4) 这次吃饭打了八折。 □

3. 买单的时候是谁付的钱?
   (1) 买单的时候是三木付的钱。 □
   (2) 买单的时候是马飞付的钱。 □

第二十四课　共计九百零二元

(3) 买单的时候是马建付的钱。　　　　　　　　□
(4) 买单的时候是王明英付的钱。　　　　　　　□

4. 结账的时候给了多少钱？找了多少钱？
 (1) 给了八百元，找了二十元。　　　　　　　□
 (2) 给了八百二十元，找了五元。　　　　　　□
 (3) 给了一千元，找了二十元。　　　　　　　□
 (4) 给了一千元，找了九十八元。　　　　　　□

第二十五课 复习(五)
Lesson Twenty-five Review (5)

一、朗读下列各组汉字,把相同的部件写在括号里并说出它的名称
Read aloud the following *Hanzi*, write the common component of each group of *Hanzi* in the bracket and tell its name

1. 菜　茶　英　(　)
2. 尝　常　(　)
3. 现　理　(　)
4. 烧　烤　烦　(　)
5. 找　打　折　接　授　(　)
6. 饮　饭　(　)
7. 红　绿　给　(　)
8. 欢　饮　(　)
9. 鸭　鸡　(　)
10. 优　就　(　)
11. 教　做　敢　(　)
12. 蒸　点　热　(　)

二、阅读理解 Reading comprehension

马太太请客吃饭

　　王明英做东,在北京饭店请客吃饭。王明英是马飞先生的太太。来吃饭的人都到了,一共五个人。他们是:三木先生、林正美小姐、马飞先生、马太太和她的儿子马建。

　　在饭店吃饭,一般(yìbān: ordinary)是先点饮料,再点菜和主食,最后(zuìhòu: finally)叫点心。

　　马太太先问大家想喝什么饮料。饮料有很多种(zhǒng:kind),茶、咖啡、啤酒等(děng:and so on)都是饮料。中国茶很有名,有红

第二十五课　复习（五）

茶和绿茶。龙井是绿茶,最有名。马建说林小姐喜欢喝龙井,马太太说正好她也喜欢喝龙井,他们就叫了龙井。三木和马飞喝咖啡。他们又(yòu:also)叫了两瓶啤酒和一瓶红酒。马建说,他妈妈和林小姐都能喝红酒。

　　点过饮料就点菜,马太太问大家喜欢吃什么。马飞说,三木喜欢吃烤鸭,这里的烤鸭很好吃。三木说林小姐也喜欢吃烤鸭,她还喜欢吃鱼。马先生喜欢吃红烧肉和家常豆腐。大家没想到点凉菜,马建说,林小姐最喜欢吃白斩鸡,北京饭店的白斩鸡很好。他们点了一只烤鸭,一条红烧鲤鱼,一个红烧肉,一个家常豆腐,一个青菜和一个白斩鸡。只有白斩鸡是凉菜,其他(qítā:other)都是热菜。

　　马太太要点主食的时候,林小姐说,她已经吃饱了,不吃主食了。马先生知道三木喜欢吃饺子,就点了一斤。他说他太太是南方人,喜欢吃米饭,就叫了一碗。马建喜欢吃面条,也叫了一碗。马先生问大家要不要叫点心,三木说,都已经吃饱了,不要叫点心了。他们只吃了米饭、饺子和面条,没有吃点心。

　　吃过饭就结账,马建负责买单。打过八折以后(yǐhòu:after),饭费(fèi:cost)共计九百零二元。马建给了一千元,服务员找给他九十八元。林小姐说:"谢谢买单的",马建说,这是他妈妈的钱,他是替他妈妈买单的。

三、根据阅读内容完成句子 Complete the following sentences according to what you read above

1. 在饭店吃饭,一般是先点_____,再点_____和_____,最后叫_____。
2. 饮料有_____种,茶、咖啡、啤酒等_____饮料。
3. 中国茶很有名,有_____茶和_____茶。龙井是_____茶,最_____。
4. 他们又叫了两_____啤酒和一_____红酒。
5. 马太太和林小姐都能_____红酒。
6. 他们点了一_____烤鸭,一_____红烧鲤鱼,一_____红烧肉,一_____家常豆腐,一_____青菜和一_____白斩鸡。白斩鸡是_____菜,其他都是_____菜。

7. 他们只_____了米饭、饺子和面条,没有_____点心。

8. 打过_____以后,饭费_____902元。马建_____了一千元,服务员_____给他98元。

四、写一篇短文说说你在饭店吃中餐的情况 Write an essay about your having Chinese food in a restaurant

第二十六课　马总正在开会
Lesson Twenty-six　General Manager Ma is at a Meeting

一、复习并记住下列部件的名称 Review the names of the following *Hanzi* components, and learn them by heart

　　⺮(等)　⻊(路)　予(预)　页(顺)

二、把下列各组汉字中相同的部件写在括号里 Write the common component of each group of *Hanzi* in the bracket

　　1. 约　的　(　)
　　2. 路　客　(　)
　　3. 周　结　(　)
　　4. 秘　和　(　)
　　5. 男　累　(　)
　　6. 预　顺　题　烦　(　)

三、说出下列部件的名称 Tell the names of the following *Hanzi* components

　　页(烦)　必(秘)　辶(迎)　冂(周)

四、把下列汉字的义符写在括号里 Write the meaning components of the following *Hanzi* in the brackets

　　起(　)　题(　)　办(　)

五、把下列各组词语中读音相同的汉字写在括号里 Write the homophonic *Hanzi* in each group of *zi*-group in the bracket

　　1. 里面　经理(　,　)

2. 客气　汽车（　，　）
3. 开会　优惠（　，　）
4. 男人　南方（　，　）

六、完成下面的句子 Complete the following sentences

1. 我路_____这里，顺便来看_____马总。
2. 马总_____开会，您能等_____吗？
3. 您汉语说_____真好，是在哪儿学_____？
4. 您请里_____坐。
5. 您就_____我小周吧。
6. 我的名字是_____的_____，不是_____的_____。

七、翻译下面的句子 Translate the following sentences

1. 汉译英 Chinese to English
   (1) 我路过这里，顺便来看看我的同学。
   (2) 您不必客气。
   (3) 您请会客室里坐。
   (4) 你可以叫我小王。

2. 英译汉 English to Chinese
   (1) General Manager Ma is making a phone call.
   (2) They are at a meeting.
   (3) I heard Mr. Wang is not very healthy. Do visit him if you are passing by (his home).
   (4) Please say hello to Mr. Ma when you see him.

八、用竖线把下列句子的主体和述体隔开 Separate the topic and the comment of each sentence with a vertical line after the models

例 Models：
1. 我们｜是学习汉语的学生。
2. 马太太｜请林小姐吃饭。

1. 林正美是韩国人。

2. 王师母不是中国人。
3. 马先生和马太太有两个儿子。
4. 王教授没有女儿。
5. 马飞家在长安街。
6. 他们身体都很好。
7. 北京烤鸭很有名。
8. 龙井茶很好喝。
9. 这家饭店的烤鸭不好吃。
10. 马阳在北京大学学习中文专业。
11. 三木在北京语言大学学了四年汉语。
12. 有人不喜欢吃饺子。
13. 您汉语说得真好。
14. 马太太一家和他们的朋友在北京饭店吃饭了。
15. 马总办公室的秘书姓周。
16. 马太太叫王明英。
17. 马家四口人。
18. 今天星期六。
19. 中午不能喝酒。
20. 下回我做东。
21. 鲤鱼要清蒸的还是要红烧的?
22. 面条、饺子、包子我都爱吃。

九、阅读理解 Reading comprehension

"周南"还是"周男"?

马飞是一家公司的总经理,人们都叫他"马总"。"马总"就是"马飞总经理"。三木是日本人,在北京的一家韩国公司工作,和马总早就认识了,他们是老朋友。

一天,三木路过马总的公司,就想顺便去看看马总。到了马总的公司,他见到了马总办公室的秘书。秘书对她说,马总正在开会。她问三木是不是预约了,能不能等等。三木说,他没有预约,可以等一会儿。秘书对三木很客气,请他到里面的会客室里坐,给他倒(dào: pour)水喝。

三木问秘书的姓名,秘书告诉(gàosu:tell)他,她姓周,叫周男。三木以为"周男"的"男"是"南方"的男,就问:周秘书是南方人吧?周秘书说:"我是南京人。"南京在南方。她知道三木以为她名字中的"男"是"南方"的"南",就说:"不过我的名字是'男人'的'男',不是'南方'的'南'。"女人的名字为什么(wèishénme:for what reason)用"男人"的"男"字?周男的名字是她父母起的,她父母希望(xīwàng:wish)她像男人。

周秘书说,三木先生汉语说得真好;三木先生说,周秘书的名字起得真好。

十、根据阅读内容完成句子 Complete the following sentences according to what you read above

1. _____ 就是"马飞总经理"。
2. 三木_____,就想_____。
3. 三木在马总的公司见到了_____。
4. 马总办公室的秘书____周,____周男。
5. 周男的____是____的____,不是____的____。
6. 周秘书_____很客气,请他到里面的_____,_____倒水喝。
7. 周男的父母希望她_____。
8. 周秘书说,三木汉语_____;三木说,周男的名字_____。

第二十七课　让您久等了
Lesson Twenty-seven　Sorry for Having Kept You Waiting So Long

一、复习并记住下列部件的名称 Review the names of the following *Hanzi* components and learn them by heart

　　工(项)　牛(件)　贝(贺)

二、把下列各组汉字中相同的部件写在括号里 Write the common component of each group of Hanzi in the bracket

　　1. 设　没　（　）
　　2. 签　等　（　）
　　3. 判　刚　到　（　）
　　4. 贺　贵　员　（　）

三、说出下列部件的名称 Tell the names of the following *Hanzi* components

　　⺮(签)　车(软)　上(让)　页(项)　刂(刚)　攵(散)　(合)给
　　办(协)　欠(软)　目(看)

四、把下列汉字的义符写在括号里 Write the meaning components of the following *Hanzi* in the brackets

　　谈(　)　订(　)　散(　)　签(　)　判(　)　协(　)　议(　)

五、把下列各组词语中读音相同的汉字写在括号里 Write the homophonic *Hanzi* in each group of *zi*-group in the bracket

　　1. 董事　不是　（　，　）
　　2. 软件　看见　（　，　）

3. 等于　鲤鱼（　，　）
4. 项目　向东（　，　）
5. 项目　三木（　，　）
6. 签订　一定（　，　）
7. 协议　一千元（　，　）
8. 合同　你和我（　，　）

六、完成下面的句子 Complete the following sentences

1. 三木先生来_____。
2. 太好_____！
3. 让你久等_____。
4. 您散会_____吗？
5. 在那里谈_____几个合作项目。
6. 我刚_____上海回来。
7. 谈判_____怎么样？
8. 谈_____非常好。

七、用竖线前后的词语做主体和述体造句 Make a sentence with the given *zi*-groups, with that on the left of the vertical line as the topic and that on the right as the comment after the models

例 Models：

1. 马飞家｜长安街
　　马飞家在长安街。
2. 林小姐｜最喜欢
　　林小姐最喜欢吃白斩鸡。

1. 王师母｜美国人
2. 王同｜王教授的儿子
3. 今天｜生日
4. 马太太｜王明英
5. 马飞的大儿子｜马建
6. 三木和林正美｜韩国公司

7. 我们│去过
8. 马建│喜欢
9. 二十分钟│到
10. 马总│开会

八、阅读理解 Reading comprehension

这是大喜事

　　三木到马总公司的时候,马总正在开会。三木在会客室里等他。马总散会以后(yǐhòu: after)就来见他的老朋友。他说:"对不起,没想到你来,让你久等了。"三木说:"我没有预约,路过这里,顺便来看看您。"他问马太太好。三木说,他昨天刚从上海回来;他在那里和一家公司谈了几个合作项目,都是关于软件设计的。马总知道三木去过上海了,他问谈判谈得怎么样。三木说,谈得很好,下周就要签订合作协议了。林董事长要从韩国到上海签字。马总听了很高兴,他说:"这是大喜事,祝贺你们。"

九、根据阅读内容完成句子 Complete the following sentences according to what you read above

1. 三木到马总的公司_____时候,马总_____开会。
2. 没想_____你来,让你久等_____。
3. 马总听说三木去_____了。
4. 三木昨天刚_____上海回来,他在那里和一家公司谈_____几个合作项目。
5. 三木在上海谈判谈_____很好,下周就要签合作协议_____。
6. 林董事长要_____韩国_____上海签字。

第二十八课 这是互利双赢的好项目
Lesson Twenty-eight This is a Mutually Beneficial Win-win Project

一、复习并记住下列部件的名称 Review the names of the following *Hanzi* components and learn them by heart

礻(社) 衤(补) 弓(强) 巾(市) 宀(定)

二、把下列各组汉字中相同的部件写在括号里 Write the common component of each group of *Hanzi* in the bracket

1. 社 视 (　)
2. 发 双 (　)
3. 短 知 (　)
4. 功 项 (　)

三、说出下列部件的名称 Tell the names of the following *Hanzi* components

刂(利) 见(视) 豆(短) 重(董) 王(望) 取(最)
力(男) 宀(定) 廾(算) 目(算)

四、把下列各组词语中读音相同的汉字写在括号里 Write the homophonic *Hanzi* in each group of *zi*-group in the bracket

1. 互利 能力 (　,　)
2. 希望 西面 (　,　)
3. 水平 酒瓶 (　,　)
4. 成功 办公 工作 (　,　,　)
5. 市场 重视 教室 不是 (　,　,　,　)

第二十八课　这是互利双赢的好项目

五、完成下面的句子 Complete the following sentences

1. 计算机_____市_____很大。
2. 林董事长要我_____他_____您问好。
3. 这是个互利双赢_____好项目。
4. 林董事长很重视上海_____合作项目。
5. 希望他这_____也来北京。
6. 他会来_____。
7. 董事长夫人_____来看她的女儿。

六、用竖线把下列句子的主体和述体隔开 Separate the topic and the comment of each sentence with a vertical line

1. 计算机软件市场很大。
2. 你们的市场开发能力很强。
3. 这家上海公司的软件设计水平不错。
4. 双方合作可以取长补短。
5. 我想一定能成功。

七、用双竖线把分句隔开,用单竖线分句的主体和述体隔开 Separate the clauses in each sentence with a vertical parallel and the topic and comment in each clause with a vertical line

1. 我们刚散会,我就来。
2. 这是大喜事,我祝贺你们!
3. 这是我妈给我的钱,我妈的钱比我多。
4. 中餐很便宜,下次请你们吃西餐。
5. 会客室在里面,您请里面坐。
6. 我路过这里,顺便来看看马总。
7. 我昨天刚从上海回来,在那里谈了几个合作项目。
8. 谈得非常好,林董事长下周来签协议。

八、阅读理解 Reading comprehension

林董事长要来北京看望马总

马总和三木在马总公司的会客室里谈话。三木告诉(gàosu: tell)马总,林董事长要到上海签订合作协议,还要三木替他向马总问好。马总和林董事长是老朋友,他希望林董事长这次也来北京。三木说,林董事长要来北京看望马总,董事长夫人也来,她要来看她的女儿。她的女儿就是林正美。

马总和三木也谈到韩国公司在上海的合作项目。这是一个关于计算机软件设计的项目。三木说,这家上海公司的软件设计水平很高,可是市场开发能力不强。马总说:"你们的市场开发能力很强,双方合作可以取长补短。"三木告诉马总,林董事长认为(rènwéi: consider)这是个互利双赢的好项目,所以(suǒyǐ :so)非常重视。马总说:"计算机软件市场很大,林董事长很有远见。"

九、根据阅读内容完成句子 Complete the following sentences according to what you read above

1. 这家上海公司的软件设计水平很高,_____市场开发能力_____。
2. 马总说:双方合作可以_____,他希望双方合作_____。
3. 林董事长认为这是个_____的好项目,所以_____。
4. 马总认为:计算机软件市场_____,林董事长很有_____。
5. 林董事长的女儿就是_____。
6. 林董事长要到上海签订_____。
7. 林董事长要来北京_____。
8. 董事长夫人要来北京_____。

第二十九课　贵客到了
Lesson Twenty-nine　The Distinguished Guest is Arriving

一、复习并记住下列部件的名称 Review the names of the following *Hanzi* components, and learn them by heart

　　彡(须)　耳(职)　力(加)

二、把下列各组汉字中相同的部件写在括号里 Write the common component of each group of *Hanzi* in the bracket

　　1. 参　须（　）
　　2. 地　场（　）
　　3. 职　识（　）
　　4. 照　绍（　）
　　5. 乱　话（　）
　　6. 爸　吧（　）
　　7. 情　忙　快（　）

三、说出下列部件的名称 Tell the names of the following *Hanzi* components

　　父(爸)　厶(参)　非(辈)　⺮(笑)　包(饱)　忄(情)　王(玩)
　　元(玩)　车(辈)　力(男)　勹(句)　工(式)

四、把下列汉字的义符写在括号里 Write the meaning components of the following *Hanzi* in the brackets

　　1. 爸（　）
　　2. 感（　）
　　3. 情（　）
　　4. 照（　）

5. 担（　）
6. 地（　）

五、完成下面的句子 Complete the following sentences

1. 我先生回来说_____,这是个_____消息。
2. 他们_____请您和马先生吃饭,请马建和马阳_____参加。
3. 在北京我们是_____,必须_____我们做东。
4. 我爸爸、妈妈这次_____北京,_____专门来感谢您和马先生_____。
5. 我的实习期满_____。
6. 马建听说你要回国,_____担心你不回_____呢。
7. 我一辈子_____要在中国工作。
8. 马太太真会_____玩笑!

六、用双竖线把分句隔开,用单竖线分句的主体和述体隔开 Separate the clauses in each sentence with a vertical parallel and the topic and comment in each clause with a vertical line

1. 我以前不喜欢吃面食,现在也喜欢了,面条、包子我都爱吃。
2. 三木说:"他没有预约,路过这里,顺便来看看马总。"
3. 三木刚从上海回来,他在那里和一家公司谈了几个合作项目,都是关于计算机软件设计的。
4. 马总听了很高兴,他说,这是大喜事,祝贺你们。
5. 马太太不必客气,我爸爸、妈妈这次来北京,是专门来感谢您和马先生的。
6. 这一年多以来,你们总是热情地关心我,给了我很多照顾。

七、阅读理解 Reading comprehension

林小姐一辈子都要在中国工作

　　林小姐来到了马家,马太太热情地欢迎她。

　　林小姐告诉(gàosu:tell)马太太,她爸爸和妈妈要来北京。马太太说:"这是个好消息。听说你父母要来北京,我们都非常高兴。"

　　林小姐说,她爸爸和妈妈要请马太太一家人吃饭。马太太说:

第二十九课　贵客到了

"怎么能让他们请客？在北京我们是主人，必须由我们做东。"林小姐请马太太不要客气。她说，马太太和马先生总是热情地关心她，给了她很多照顾，她父母这次来北京，是专门来向马太太和马先生表示(biǎoshì:express)感谢的。马太太说，他们关心和照顾林小姐是应该的。她还问林小姐是不是要和她父母一起回国。林小姐说，她现在是在公司实习，实习期已经满了。回国以后还要再来，再来就是正式职工了。

谈话的时候，马太太主动(zhǔdòng:take the initiative)说起了马建和林小姐的关系。她说，马建担心林小姐回国以后就不回来了。林小姐说，她一辈子都要在中国工作。她这样说，是想让马建放心(fàngxīn:feel relieved)。马太太说："马建听到你这句话，一定要高兴死了！"她这样说，是想让林小姐知道，马建非常喜欢她，很希望她一辈子都在中国工作。林小姐听了马太太的话，心里非常高兴，嘴(zuǐ:mouth)里却(què:but)说："马太太真会开玩笑。"

八、根据阅读内容完成句子 Complete the following sentences according to what you read above

1. 听说林小姐的父母要_____，马家的人都_____。
2. 林小姐对马太太说，她爸爸和妈妈要_____。
3. 马太太对林小姐说，不能让林小姐的父母请客，在北京他们_____，必须由他们_____。
4. 林小姐说，她父母这次来北京，是专门来向马太太和马先生_____。
5. 马太太说，他们关心和照顾林小姐_____。
6. 林小姐现在是在公司_____，_____期已经_____。
7. 林小姐回国以后还要_____，_____就是_____了。
8. 谈话的时候，马太太主动说起了_____。
9. 马建担心林小姐回国以后_____。
10. 林小姐说，她_____都要在中国工作。
11. 马建非常_____林小姐，很希望林小姐_____都在中国工作。

第三十课 复习(六)
Lesson Thirty Review (6)

一、朗读下列各组汉字,把相同的部件写在括号里并说出它的名称
Read aloud the following *Hanzi*, write the common component of each group of *Hanzi* in the bracket and tell it's name

1. 安 家 实 室 客 宜 ( )
2. 单 关 美 总 ( )
3. 菜 茶 英 董 ( )
4. 老 教 ( )
5. 六 市 京 高 离 ( )
6. 尝 常 ( )
7. 有 友 ( )
8. 签 等 算 笑 ( )
9. 次 凉 ( )
10. 软 较 辅 ( )
11. 得 很 街 ( )
12. 功 项 ( )
13. 烧 烤 烦 ( )
14. 钟 钱 ( )
15. 林 机 ( )
16. 体 做 候 便 件 健 位 像 优 ( )
17. 给 结 经 绍 约 红 绿 ( )
18. 短 知 ( )
19. 饮 饭 饺 ( )
20. 社 视 祝 ( )
21. 找 打 折 接 授 ( )
22. 汉 没 消 海 清 酒 沙 ( )

46

23. 地 场　（　）
24. 情 忙 快　（　）
25. 说 谈 语 谁 谢 该 设 计 让 认 议　（　）
26. 鸡 欢 双 对　（　）
27. 现 理　（　）
28. 判 刚 到 利　（　）
29. 那 哪 都　（　）
30. 教 做 敢 散 数　（　）
31. 开 算　（　）
32. 蒸 点 热　（　）
33. 会 么 去 公　（　）
34. 定 是　（　）
35. 句 包　（　）
36. 道 过 远 近 这 还 迎　（　）
37. 周 用　（　）

二、阅读理解 Reading comprehension

林董事长和夫人要来北京

三木和林正美在北京的一家韩国公司工作,这家韩国公司的总部(zǒngbù:general headquarters)在韩国,董事长就是林正美的父亲。

三木去了一次上海,和上海的一家公司谈成了几个合作项目,都是关于计算机软件设计的。三木告诉(gàosu:tell)马总,他们的林董事长非常重视这项合作,认为(rènwéi:consider)这是个互利双赢的好项目,要亲自(qīnzì:personally)到上海签订合作协议;林董事长在上海签字以后要来北京看望马总,董事长夫人也来,她要来看她的女儿林正美。

林董事长和马总是好朋友。马建在韩国学习的时候,林董事长和夫人非常关心他,给了他很多照顾。林正美在北京实习,马总和马太太也都热情地关心和照顾她。马建和林正美早就成了好朋友,他们都非常喜欢对方(duìfāng:the opposite side)。

林正美到马家告诉马太太她父母要来北京的消息。她说,马太太和马先生总是热情地关心她,给了她很多照顾。她父母这次来北京,要请他们一家人吃饭,向他们表示(biǎoshì:express)感谢。

　　林正美要和她父母一起(yìqǐ:together)回韩国。她对马太太说:她回国以后还要再来,一辈子都要在中国工作。马太太也很喜欢林正美,她知道林正美和马建都喜欢对方,感到非常高兴。她对林正美说,马建担心她回国以后不再回来,要是(yàoshi:if)知道她一辈子都要在中国工作,一定要高兴死了。她想让林正美知道,她一定支持(zhīchí:support)他们。

三、根据阅读内容完成句子 Complete the following sentences according to what you read above

1. 三木去了一次_____,和_____的一家公司谈成了几个合作项目,都是_____计算机软件设计的。
2. 林董事长非常重视这_____合作,认为这是个互利双赢的_____。
3. 林董事长在上海签字以后要来北京_____,董事长夫人_____,她要来_____。
4. 马建和林正美早就成了_____,他们都_____对方。
5. 林正美到马家告诉马太太_____。
6. 林正美的父母这次来北京,要请马太太_____吃饭,向他们表示_____。
7. 林正美要和她父母一起_____,她回国以后_____。
8. 马太太想让林正美知道,她_____支持他们。

四、写一篇短文谈谈你的工作或生活 Write an essay about your work or life

附录　练习题答案
Appendix　Key to the Exercises

第十六课　马先生在家吗？

复习并记住下列部件的名称

扌(打)　手部旁
纟(给)　纟部旁
辶(还)　走部框
文(这)　文部心

把下列各组汉字中相同的部件写在括号里

1. 打　接　授　(扌)
2. 给　经　绍　(纟)
3. 吗　码　(马)

说出下列部件的名称

几(机)　几部边
人(认)　人部边
建(健)　建部边
生(姓)　生部边
你(您)　你部头

把下列汉字的义符写在括号里

海(氵)　说(讠)　打(扌)　授(扌)　想(心)　他(亻)
她(女)　吗(口)　叫(口)　远(辶)　林(木)　机(木)

完成下面的句子

1. 马先生在不在家？
2. 马先生不在家。
3. 您可以给他办公室打电话。
4. 您可以打他办公室的电话。
5. 您打他的手机吧。

49

6. 我没有他公司的电话号码。
7. 他的手机号码是幺三零五二四六六七八八。

把字词连成句子

1. 呢 没 还 回 马先生 家
   马先生还没回家呢。
2. 吗 三木先生 韩国 去 回 了
   三木先生回韩国去了吗?
3. 您 打 的 他 吧 电话 办公室
   您打他办公室的电话吧。
4. 打 您 的 他 吧 手机
   您打他的手机吧。
5. 他 没 手机 接 的 人
   他的手机没人接。

翻译下面的词语和句子

1. 汉译英

   (1) 韩国公司 Korean company

   (2) 电话号码 telephone number

   (2) 手机号码 mobile phone number

   (3) 打他的手机 call him by his mobile phone

   (4) 打他办公室的电话 call him by his office telephone

   (5) 公司的电话号码 company's telephone number

2. 英译汉

   (1) He went to an American company.
       他去了一家美国公司。
   (2) You'd better phone his company's telephone.
       您打他公司的电话吧。
   (3) You can call him mobile phone.
       您可以给他打手机。
   (4) I don't have his mobile phone number.
       我没有他的手机号码。

根据阅读内容选择正确答案,在正确答案后面的方框内打√

1. 谁给马先生家打电话了?
   (1) 王老师给马先生家打电话了。 ☐
   (2) 王太太给马先生家打电话了。 ☐
   (3) 三木先生给马先生家打电话了。 ☐
   (4) 林正美给马先生家打电话了。 ☑

2. 三木打给马先生的电话是谁接的？
   (1) 三木打给马先生的电话是马太太接的。 ☑
   (2) 三木打给马先生的电话是马先生的儿子接的。 ☐
   (3) 三木打给马先生的电话是马先生的女儿接的。 ☐
   (4) 三木打给马先生的电话是马先生接的。 ☐

第十七课　请你替我向她问好

复习并记住下列部件的名称

火(烦)　火部旁
车(辅)　车部旁
饣(饭)　食部旁

把下列各组汉字中相同的部件写在括号里

1. 忙　快　(忄)
2. 麻　康　(广)
3. 教　做　敢　(攵)

说出下列部件的名称

口(问)　口部心
口(向)　口部心
林(麻)　林部心
广(麻)　广部框
广(康)　广部框
辶(过)　走部框
辶(远)　走部框

把下列汉字的音符写在括号里

1. 吗 (马)
2. 码 (马)
3. 们 (门)
4. 问 (门)
5. 字 (子)
6. 机 (几)
7. 认 (人)
8. 什 (十)
9. 您 (你)

完成下面的句子

1. 请你<u>替</u>我向王教授问好。
2. 白天工作很<u>忙</u>,晚<u>上</u>还要学习。
3. 你是个<u>大</u>忙人,我不<u>敢</u>麻烦你。
4. 我妈妈要<u>给</u>你打电话,她想<u>请</u>你吃饭。

把字词连成句子

1. 不 了 见 好 久
   好久不见了。
2. 工作 吗 忙 你
   你工作忙吗?
3. 白天 不 工作 忙,很 工作 晚上 忙
   白天工作不忙,晚上工作很忙。
4. 不 他 敢 你 麻烦
   他不敢麻烦你。
5. 要 马太太 林小姐 打 给 电话
   马太太要给林小姐打电话。
6. 请 马太太 要 林小姐 午饭 吃
   马太太要请林小姐吃午饭。

根据阅读内容选择正确答案,在正确答案后面的方框内打√

1. 马建和林正美是在哪儿认识的?
   (1) 他们是在中国认识的。 ☐
   (2) 他们是在日本认识的。 ☐
   (3) 他们是在美国认识的。 ☐
   (4) 他们是在韩国认识的。 ☑

2. 马建在哪儿学习过?
   (1) 马建在英国学习过。 ☐
   (2) 马建在美国学习过。 ☐
   (3) 马建在韩国学习过。 ☑
   (4) 马建在日本学习过。 ☐

3. 马建给林正美打电话说什么了?
   (1) 他很想她。 ☐
   (2) 他想见她。 ☐
   (3) 他想给林正美辅导汉语。 ☐
   (4) 他妈妈想请林正美吃饭。 ☑

4. 听说(tīngshuō:be told)马建的妈妈要请她吃饭,林正美同意(tóngyì:agree)了吗?
   (1) 她同意了。 ☑
   (2) 她没同意。 ☐

第十八课　我想请你吃午饭

复习并记住下列部件的名称

矢（知）　矢部旁

灬（点）　火部底

扌（用）　手部心

冂（用）　用部框

把下列各组汉字中相同的部件写在括号里

1. 较　辅　（车）
2. 点　店　（占）
3. 间　问　们　（门）
4. 怎　作　昨　（乍）

说出下列部件的名称

丷（关）　八部头

天（关）　天部底

小（系）　小部底

心（怎）　心部底

匕（比）　匕部边

把下列汉字的义符写在括号里

1. 吃（口）
2. 饭（饣）
3. 店（广）
4. 点（灬）

完成下面的句子

1. 我和我先生想请你和三木先生吃午饭。
2. 星期六中午十二点。
3. 在哪儿？
4. 在北京饭店。
5. 你知道北京饭店在哪儿吗？
6. 我可以问人。

把字词连成句子

1. 你　吗　忙　最近
   你最近忙吗？

53

2. 最近 吗 好 身体 马太太
   马太太最近身体好吗?
3. 你 北京饭店 哪儿 在 知道 吗
   你知道北京饭店在哪儿吗?
4. 十二点 中午 星期六
   星期六中午十二点。
5. 见 星期六
   星期六见。

翻译下面的词语和句子

1. 汉译英
   (1) 儿子和女儿
       sons and daughters
   (2) 王明英和马飞
       Wang Mingying and Ma Fei
   (3) 北京饭店很大。
       Beijing Hotel is very big.
   (4) 今天中午我们请你吃午饭。
       We invite you to lunch today.
   (5) 马总八点来公司。
       General Manager Ma comes to the company at eight o'clock.
2. 英译汉
   (1) Japan and America.
       日本和美国
   (2) What time do you have lunch?
       你几点吃午饭?
   (3) Mrs. Ma invited us to lunch yesterday.
       马太太昨天请我吃午饭了。
   (4) It's very nice!
       太好了!

根据阅读内容选择正确答案,在正确答案后面的方框内打√

1. 王明英请谁吃饭?
   (1) 王明英请马飞的老师吃饭。 ☐
   (2) 王明英请王教授吃饭。 ☐
   (3) 王明英请王同吃饭。 ☐
   (4) 王明英请三木和林正美吃饭。 ☑
2. 王明英请他们在哪儿吃饭?
   (1) 王明英请他们在家吃饭。 ☐
   (2) 王明英请他们在公司吃饭。 ☐

(3) 王明英请他们在北京饭店吃饭。 ☑
(4) 王明英请他们在办公室吃饭。 ☐

3. 他们什么时候在北京饭店吃饭？
 (1) 星期五中午十二点。 ☐
 (2) 星期六中午十二点。 ☑
 (3) 星期日中午十二点。 ☐
 (4) 星期二中午十二点。 ☐

4. 北京饭店在哪儿？
 (1) 北京饭店在天安门广场。 ☐
 (2) 北京饭店在北京大学。 ☐
 (3) 北京饭店在北京语言大学。 ☐
 (4) 北京饭店在长安街。 ☑

5. 林小姐知道北京饭店在哪儿吗？
 (1) 她知道。 ☐
 (2) 她不知道。 ☑

第十九课　北京饭店在哪儿？

复习并记住下列部件的名称

钅（钟）　金部旁

立（站）　立部旁

走（走）　走部底

把下列各组汉字中相同的部件写在括号里

1. 分　公（ 八 ）
2. 南　幸（ 𢆉 ）
3. 多　名（ 夕 ）
4. 钟　贵（ 中 ）
5. 应　兴（ 䒑 ）
6. 那　哪　都（ 阝 ）
7. 最　星　是　白（ 日 ）

说出下列部件的名称

八（分）　八部头

八（共）　八部底

十（南）　十部头

十（早）　十部底

亠（离）　六部头

西（要）　西部头

气（汽）　气部边
免（晚）　免部边
中（钟）　中部边
不（还）　不部心
口（可）　口部心

把下列汉字的义符写在括号里

1. 汽（氵）
2. 钟（钅）
3. 站（立）
4. 烦（火）
5. 辅（车）
6. 问（口）

完成下面的句子

1. <u>请问</u>,北京饭店在哪儿？
2. 去北京饭店<u>怎么</u>走？
3. 您可以从这儿<u>向西</u>。
4. 北京饭店<u>离</u>这儿远不远？
5. 要是坐公共汽车,<u>多长</u>时间能到？
6. 打的比较快,十分钟就到。

把字词连成句子

1. 哪儿　在　天安门
   天安门在哪儿？
2. 在　北京语言大学　东面　北京大学
   北京语言大学在北京大学东面。
3. 远　这儿　天安门广场　离　不
   天安门广场离这儿不远。
4. 就　南面　在　车站
   车站就在南面。
5. 这儿　去　从　北京大学,就　十分钟　到　打的
   从这儿去北京大学,打的十分钟就到。

根据阅读内容选择正确答案,在正确答案后面的方框内打✓

1. 林正美在去哪儿的路上问路？
   (1) 林正美在去北京大学的路上问路。　☐
   (2) 林正美在去北京饭店的路上问路。　✓
2. 林正美问路问了几个人？
   (1) 林正美问路问了两个人。　✓

(2) 林正美问路问了三个人。 ☐

3. 北京饭店离问路的地方(dìfang: place)远不远?
　　(1) 北京饭店离问路的地方非常远。 ☐
　　(2) 北京饭店离问路的地方不太远。 ☑

4. 从问路的地方去北京饭店,坐公共汽车多长时间能到?
　　(1) 坐公共汽车二十分钟能到。 ☑
　　(2) 坐公共汽车十分钟能到。 ☐

5. 从问路的地方去北京饭店,打的多长时间能到?
　　(1) 打的十分钟能到。 ☑
　　(2) 打的二十分钟能到。 ☐

第二十课　复习(四)

说出下列部件的名称

1

耂(老)	老部头
ナ(有)	手部头
𠂊(看)	手部头
亠(离)	六部头
宀(实)	安部头
丷(关)	八部头

2

亻(你)	人部旁
讠(话)	言部旁
女(姓)	女部旁
氵(汉)	水部旁
忄(快)	心部旁
木(机)	木部旁
火(烦)	火部旁
车(辅)	车部旁
饣(饭)	食部旁
扌(打)	手部旁
纟(给)	纟部旁
钅(钟)	金部旁
立(站)	立部旁
矢(知)	矢部旁

3

| 刂(到) | 刀部边 |
| 匕(比) | 匕部边 |

建(健)　建部边
生(姓)　生部边

4

木(亲)　木部底
厶(去)　厶部底
走(走)　走部底
灬(点)　火部底
匕(老)　匕部底
大(奖)　大部底
心(想)　心部底
生(星)　生部底

5

辶(还)　走部框
冂(用)　用部框

6

扌(用)　手部心
文(这)　文部心

根据阅读内容选择正确答案,在正确答案后面的方框内打√

1. 马飞和三木常常他们互相打电话,是因为(yīnwèi:because)他们是老朋友。　□
   马飞和三木常常他们互相打电话,是因为要互相问好。　√
   马飞和三木常常他们互相打电话,是因为要互相请吃饭。　□

2. 三木给马飞家打电话,是因为他不知道马飞办公室的电话号码。　□
   三木给马飞家打电话,是因为马飞办公室的电话没人接。　√
   三木给马飞家打电话,是因为他要向马太太问好。　□

3. 马建给林正美打电话,是为了(wèile:for the sake of)问三木的手机号码。　□
   马建给林正美打电话,是为了向林正美问好。　□
   马建给林正美打电话,是为了告诉(gàosu:tell)她,他妈妈要请她吃饭。　√

4. 林正美很喜欢(xǐhuan:like)马建。　√
   林正美不喜欢马建。　□

5. 王明英和马飞请林正美和三木吃晚饭。　□
   王明英和马飞请林正美和三木吃早饭。　□
   王明英和马飞请林正美和三木吃午饭。　√

6. 他们吃午饭的时间是星期六上午十一点。　□
   他们吃午饭的时间是星期天下午两点。　□
   他们吃午饭的时间是星期六中午十二点。　√

附录 练习题答案

第二十一课 你们喝什么饮料？

复习并记住下列部件的名称

艹(茶)　艹部头
米(料)　米部旁
欠(欢)　欠部边
酉(酒)　酉部边
采(菜)　采部底

把下列各组汉字中相同的部件写在括号里

1. 菜　茶　英　(艹)
2. 红　绿　给　(纟)
3. 饮　饭　(饣)
4. 饮　欢　(欠)
5. 茶　亲　(朩)
6. 务　办　(力)

说出下列部件的名称

纟(绿)　纟部旁
饣(饮)　食部旁
工(红)　工部边
非(啡)　非部边
欠(饮)　欠部边

把下列汉字的义符写在括号里

酒(氵)　茶(艹)　菜(艹)　料(米)　喝(口)　欢(欠)

把下列各组词语中读音相同的汉字写在括号里

1. 马飞　号码 (马,码)
2. 中国　分钟 (中,钟)
3. 星期　七天 (期,七)
4. 十九　白酒 (九,酒)
5. 十个　时候 (十,时)
6. 在家　再见 (在,再)
7. 不是　办公室 (是,室)

完成下面的句子

1. 你们喝<u>什么</u>饮料？
2. 您喝茶<u>还是</u>喝咖啡？

59

3. 你们喜欢红茶还是绿茶？
4. 马太太喜欢喝绿茶。
5. 来两瓶啤酒。

翻译下面的词语和句子

1. 汉译英 Chinese to English

　　(1) 好(hǎo)吃 delicious

　　(2) 吃饭 have a meal

　　(3) 喝酒 drink wine

　　(4) 龙井茶很有名。Longjing tea is very famous.

　　(5) 林小姐喜欢吃中国菜。Miss Lin likes eating Chinese food.

　　(6) 马太太不喜欢喝红茶。Mrs.Ma doesn't like to drink black tea.

2. 英译汉

　　(1) Would you like to drink beer?

　　　你喝啤酒吗？

　　(2) What kind of drink would you like?

　　　你喝什么饮料？

　　(3) Would you like to drink tea or coffee?

　　　你喝茶还是咖啡？

　　(4) Is Longjing tea black tea or green tea?

　　　龙井茶是红茶还是绿茶？

　　(5) Does Mr. Ma like drinking black tea or green tea?

　　　马先生喜欢喝红茶,还是绿茶？

根据阅读内容选择正确答案,在正确答案后面的方框内打√

1. 林小姐和马太太喝什么饮料？
　　(1) 林小姐喝茶,马太太喝咖啡。☐
　　(2) 林小姐喝咖啡,马太太喝茶。☐
　　(3) 林小姐和马太太都喝咖啡。☐
　　(4) 林小姐和马太太都喝茶。☑

2. 林小姐和马太太喜欢喝什么茶？
　　(1) 林小姐喜欢喝红茶,马太太喜欢喝绿茶。☐
　　(2) 林小姐喜欢喝绿茶,马太太喜欢喝红茶。☐
　　(3) 林小姐和马太太都喜欢喝绿茶。☑
　　(4) 林小姐和马太太都喜欢喝红茶。☐

3. 三木和马先生喝什么饮料？
　　(1) 三木喝啤酒,马先生喝咖啡。☐
　　(2) 三木喝咖啡,马先生喝啤酒。☐
　　(3) 三木和马先生都喝咖啡。☐
　　(4) 三木和马先生都喝啤酒。☑

4. 马太太和林小姐喝酒了吗？
   (1) 她们没喝酒。 ☐
   (2) 她们喝白酒了。 ☐
   (3) 她们喝红酒了。 ☑
   (4) 她们喝白酒和红酒了。 ☐

第二十二课　你们想吃什么菜？

复习并记住下列部件的名称

覀(要)　西部头
冫(凉)　冰部旁
鸟(鸭)　鸟部边
斤(斩)　斤部边

把下列各组汉字中相同的部件写在括号里

1. 鸡　　欢　　（又）
2. 鸭　　鸡　　（鸟）
3. 斩　　近　　（斤）
4. 清　　请　　（青）
5. 鲤　　理　　（里）
6. 凉　　习　　（冫）
7. 斩　　较　　（车）
8. 饺　　较　　（交）
9. 蒸　　点　　热　　（灬）
10. 烧　　烤　　烦　　（火）

说出下列部件的名称

氵(清)　水部旁
鱼(鲤)　鱼部边
鸟(鸡)　鸟部边
多(够)　多部边
灬(蒸)　火部底
木(条)　木部底
广(腐)　广部框

把下列汉字的义符写在括号里

鸡(鸟)　烤(火)　鲤(鱼)　清(氵)　凉(冫)　蒸(灬)

完成下面的句子

1. 这是菜单,请你<u>点</u>菜。
2. 林小姐<u>太</u>客气了。
3. 你们喜欢吃<u>什么</u>菜?
4. <u>这里的</u>烤鸭很好。
5. 要一<u>只</u>烤鸭。
6. 再要一<u>条</u>红烧鲤鱼。

翻译下面的句子

1. 汉译英

   (1) 请林小姐点菜。

     Miss Lin, order (dishes), please.

   (2) 您太客气了!

     It's very kind of you.

   (3) 你们喜欢喝什么茶?

     What kind of tea would you like?

   (4) 这里的烤鸭很好吃。

     The roast duck here is delicious.

2. 英译汉

   (1) Too many dishes.

     菜太多了。

   (2) I would like to have fish in brown sauce.

     我想要红烧鱼。

   (3) They like (eating) roast duck.

     他们喜欢吃烤鸭。

   (4) I don't like the plain boiled chicken here.

     我不喜欢吃这里的白斩鸡。

根据阅读内容选择正确答案,在正确答案后面的方框内打√

1. 林小姐喜欢吃什么?

   (1) 林小姐喜欢吃烤鸭,不喜欢吃鱼。 ☐

   (2) 林小姐不喜欢吃烤鸭,喜欢吃鱼。 ☐

   (3) 林小姐不喜欢吃烤鸭,也不喜欢吃鱼。 ☐

   (4) 林小姐喜欢吃烤鸭,也喜欢吃鱼。 ☑

2. 三木喜欢吃什么?

   (1) 三木喜欢吃烤鸭,不喜欢吃红烧肉。 ☐

   (2) 三木喜欢吃烤鸭,不喜欢吃家常豆腐。 ☐

   (3) 三木喜欢吃家常豆腐,不喜欢吃烤鸭。 ☐

   (4) 三木喜欢吃烤鸭、红烧肉和家常豆腐。 ☑

3. 他们点了什么菜？
　　(1) 他们点了烤鸭、红烧鲤鱼和青菜，没点红烧肉和白斩鸡。☐
　　(2) 他们点了烤鸭、家常豆腐和白斩鸡，没点青菜和红烧鲤鱼。☐
　　(3) 他们点了青菜和清蒸鲤鱼，没点红烧肉和白斩鸡。☐
　　(4) 他们点了烤鸭、红烧鲤鱼、红烧肉、白斩鸡、青菜和家常豆腐。✓
4. 他们点了几只烤鸭、几条鲤鱼、几个青菜？
　　(1) 他们点了一只烤鸭、两条鲤鱼、三个青菜。☐
　　(2) 他们点了两只烤鸭、三条鲤鱼、一个青菜。☐
　　(3) 他们点了三只烤鸭、两条鲤鱼、四个青菜。☐
　　(4) 他们点了一只烤鸭、一条鲤鱼、一个青菜。✓

第二十三课　你们要什么主食？

复习并记住下列部件的名称

艹(尝)　小部头
𤣩(现)　玉部边
𠂉(方)　方部底
勹(包)　包部框

把下列各组汉字中相同的部件写在括号里

1. 尝　常　(艹)
2. 碗　码　(石)
3. 现　理　(𤣩)
4. 尝　会　(云)
5. 饺　较　(交)
6. 前　豆　喜　(丷)

说出下列部件的名称

宀(方)　六部头
𤣩(理)　玉部旁
米(料)　米部旁
见(现)　见部边
包(饱)　包部边
里(理)　里部边
友(爱)　友部底
玉(国)　玉部心

把下列汉字的音符写在括号里

啡(非)　清(青)　鲤(里)　饱(包)　近(斤)　现(见)　红(工)

完成下面的句子

1. 我已经吃饱了。
2. 我已经见过王先生了。
3. 他们已经去过马先生的公司了。
4. 我好久没吃面条了。
5. 我以前不喜欢吃面食,现在也喜欢了。
6. 面条、包子、饺子我都爱吃。
7. 要不要叫点心?
8. 再要一碗米饭,一碗面条。

翻译下面的词语和句子

1. 汉译英

  (1) 去过。Have been to
  (2) 看见了。caught sight of
  (3) 他没吃过烤鸭。He has never had roast duck.
  (4) 三木吃饱了,林小姐没吃饱。Sanmu has eaten enough, but Miss lin hasn't.

2. 英译汉

  (1) Please have a taste (of sth.).
     请尝一尝。
  (2) Shall we order roast duck?
     我们要点烤鸭吗?
  (3) Southerners like (eating) rice.
     南方人喜欢吃米饭。
  (4) There are enough dishes.
     菜够了。

根据阅读内容选择正确答案,在正确答案后面的方框内打√

1. 马太太叫林小姐尝尝什么?
   (1) 马太太叫林小姐尝尝米饭。 ☐
   (2) 马太太叫林小姐尝尝点心。 ☐
   (3) 马太太叫林小姐尝尝饺子。 ☑
   (4) 马太太叫林小姐尝尝烤鸭。 ☐

2. 马太太喜欢吃什么主食?
   (1) 马太太喜欢吃饺子,不喜欢吃米饭。 ☐
   (2) 马太太喜欢吃米饭,不喜欢吃饺子。 ☐
   (3) 马太太喜欢吃面条,也喜欢吃饺子。 ☐
   (4) 米饭、饺子、包子和面条她都喜欢吃。 ☑

3. 他们点了什么主食?
   (1) 他们点了米饭、饺子、包子和面条。 ☐
   (2) 他们点了米饭,没点饺子、包子和面条。 ☐

(3) 他们点了饺子和面条,没点包子和米饭。　□
　　(4) 他们点了米饭、饺子和面条,没点包子。　☑
4. 林小姐和三木吃饱了吗?
　　(1) 林小姐吃饱了,三木没吃饱。　□
　　(2) 林小姐没吃饱,三木吃饱了。　□
　　(3) 林小姐和三木都没吃饱。　□
　　(4) 林小姐和三木都吃饱了。　☑

第二十四课　共计九百零二元

复习并记住下列部件的名称

彳(得)　彳部旁
戈(找)　戈部边
尤(优)　尤部边
戋(钱)　戋部边
攵(做)　攵部边

把下列各组汉字中相同的部件写在括号里

1. 得　很　街　(彳)
2. 买　实　(头)
3. 宜　姐　(且)
4. 南　计　早　千　(十)
5. 找　打　折　接　授　(扌)

说出下列部件的名称

钅(钱)　金部旁
扌(找)　手部旁
冫(凉)　冰部旁
尤(就)　尤部边
攵(教)　攵部边
斤(折)　斤部边
欠(次)　欠部边
食(餐)　食部底
元(远)　元部心

把下列汉字的义符写在括号里

餐(食)　找(扌)　折(扌)　钱(钅)　账(贝)

把下列各组词语中读音相同的汉字写在括号里

1. 工人　公司（工,公）
2. 工作　请坐（作,坐）
3. 北京　已经（京,经）
4. 前天　多少钱（前,钱）
5. 一百元　服务员（元,员）
6. 小时　主食　五十（时,食,十）
7. 好久　十九　白酒（久,九,酒）

完成下面的句子

1. 林小姐吃<u>得</u>很少
2. 我吃饱<u>了</u>。
3. 共计三百五十<u>元</u>。
4. 打过八五<u>折</u>了。
5. 这是我妈给我<u>的</u>钱。
6. 我妈的钱<u>比</u>我多。
7. 中餐很便<u>宜</u>。
8. 下回请你们<u>吃</u>西餐。

翻译下面的词语和句子

1. 汉译英 Chinese to English

    (1) 不便宜 not cheap

    (2) 你吃好了吗? Have you had enough?

    (3) 一共二十五元。Altogether 25 yuan

    (4) 一共多少钱? How much is it altogether?

    (5) 这个菜很贵。This dish is very expensive.

2. 英译汉 English to Chinese

    (1) Too expensive!
        太贵了!

    (2) Can I have a discount?
        能打折吗?

    (3) 15% discount.
        打八五折。

    (4) He does not like (eating) Western food.
        他不喜欢吃西餐。

    (5) Is twenty yuan enough?
        20元够不够?

附录　练习题答案

根据阅读内容选择正确答案,在正确答案后面的方框内打√

1. 这次吃饭谁做东?
   (1) 这次吃饭王明英做东。　　　　　　　　　　√
   (2) 这次吃饭马飞做东。　　　　　　　　　　□
   (3) 这次吃饭马建做东。　　　　　　　　　　□
   (4) 这次吃饭林正美做东。　　　　　　　　　□

2. 这次吃饭有优惠吗?
   (1) 这次吃饭没有优惠。　　　　　　　　　　□
   (2) 这次吃饭有九折优惠。　　　　　　　　　□
   (3) 这次吃饭打了八五折。　　　　　　　　　□
   (4) 这次吃饭打了八折。　　　　　　　　　　√

3. 买单的时候是谁付的钱?
   (1) 买单的时候是三木付的钱。　　　　　　　□
   (2) 买单的时候是马飞付的钱。　　　　　　　□
   (3) 买单的时候是马建付的钱。　　　　　　　√
   (4) 买单的时候是王明英付的钱。　　　　　　□

4. 结账的时候给了多少钱?找了多少钱?
   (1) 给了八百元,找了二十元。　　　　　　　□
   (2) 给了八百二十元,找了五元。　　　　　　□
   (3) 给了一千元,找了二十元。　　　　　　　□
   (4) 给了一千元,找了 98 元。　　　　　　　√

第二十五课　复习(五)

朗读下列各组汉字,把相同的部件写在括号里并说出它的名称

1. 菜　茶　英　　　(艹)
2. 尝　常　　　　　(⺌)
3. 现　理　　　　　(王)
4. 烧　烤　烦　　　(火)
5. 找　打　折　接　授　(扌)
6. 饮　饭　　　　　(饣)
7. 红　绿　给　　　(纟)
8. 欢　饮　　　　　(欠)
9. 鸭　鸡　　　　　(鸟)
10. 优　就　　　　　(尤)
11. 教　做　敢　　　(攵)
12. 蒸　点　热　　　(灬)

67

根据阅读内容完成句子

1. 在饭店吃饭,一般是先点<u>饮料</u>,再点菜和<u>主食</u>,最后叫<u>点心</u>。
2. 饮料有<u>很</u>多种,茶、咖啡、啤酒等都是饮料。
3. 中国茶很有名,有<u>红茶</u>和<u>绿茶</u>。龙井是<u>绿茶</u>,最有名。
4. 他们又叫了两瓶啤酒和一瓶红酒。
5. 马太太和林小姐都能喝红酒。
6. 他们点了<u>一</u>只烤鸭,一条红烧鲤鱼,一<u>个</u>红烧肉,一<u>个</u>家常豆腐,一<u>个</u>青菜和一<u>个</u>白斩鸡。白斩鸡是<u>凉菜</u>,其他都是<u>热菜</u>。
7. 他们只<u>叫</u>了米饭、饺子和面条,没有叫点心。
8. 打过<u>八</u>折以后,饭费共计 902 元。马建<u>给</u>了一千元,服务员<u>找</u>给他 98 元。

第二十六课　马总正在开会

复习并记住下列部件的名称

⺮（等）　竹部头

⻊（路）　足部旁

予（预）　予部旁

页（顺）　页部边

把下列各组汉字中相同的部件写在括号里

1. 约　　的　　（勺）
2. 路　　客　　（各）
3. 周　　结　　（吉）
4. 秘　　和　　（禾）
5. 男　　累　　（田）
6. 预　　顺　　题　　烦　　（页）

说出下列部件的名称

页（烦）　页部边

必（秘）　必部边

辶（迎）　走部框

冂（周）　用部框

把下列汉字的义符写在括号里

起（走）　题（页）　办（力）

把下列各组词语中读音相同的汉字写在括号里

1. 里面　经理　（里,理）
2. 客气　汽车　（气,汽）

3. 开会　优惠　（会,惠）
4. 男人　南方　（男,南）

完成下面的句子

1. 我<u>路</u>过这里,顺便来看看马总。
2. 马总<u>正在</u>开会,您能<u>等等</u>吗?
3. 您汉语说<u>得</u>真好,是在哪儿学<u>的</u>?
4. 您请里<u>面</u>坐。
5. 您就<u>叫</u>我小周吧。
6. 我的名字是"<u>男人</u>"的"男",不是"<u>南方</u>"的"南"。

翻译下面的句子

1. 汉译英 Chinese to English
   (1) 我路过这里,顺便来看看我的同学。I visit my classmate as I just passed by here.
   (2) 您不必客气。You are welcome.
   (3) 您请会客室里坐。Please sit in the reception room.
   (4) 你可以叫我小王。You can call me Xiao Wang.
2. 英译汉 English to Chinese
   (1) General Manager Ma is making a phone call.
   　　马总正在打电话。
   (2) They are at a meeting.
   　　他们正在开会。
   (3) I heard Mr. Wang is not very healthy. Do visit him if you are passing by (his home).
   　　我听说王先生身体不太好。你路过时请顺便去看看他。
   (4) Please say hello to Mr. Ma when you see him.
   　　碰到他请替我向马先生问好。

用竖线把下列句子的主体和述体隔开

1. 林正美｜是韩国人。
2. 王师母｜不是中国人。
3. 马先生和马太太｜有两个儿子。
4. 王教授｜没有女儿。
5. 马飞家｜在长安街。
6. 他们｜身体都很好。
7. 北京烤鸭｜很有名。
8. 龙井茶｜很好喝。
9. 这家饭店的烤鸭｜不好吃。
10. 马阳｜在北京大学学习中文专业。
11. 三木｜在北京语言大学学了四年汉语。
12. 有人｜不喜欢吃饺子。

13. 您│汉语说得真好。
14. 马太太一家和他们的朋友│在北京饭店吃饭了。
15. 马总办公室的秘书│姓周。
16. 马太太│叫王明英。
17. 马家│四口人。
18. 今天│星期六。
19. 中午│不能喝酒。
20. 下回│我做东。
21. 鲤鱼│要清蒸的还是要红烧的？
22. 面条、饺子、包子│我都爱吃。

根据阅读内容完成句子

1. 马总就是"马飞总经理"。
2. 三木路过马总的公司,就想顺便去看看马总。
3. 三木在马总的公司见到了马总办公室的秘书。
4. 马总办公室的秘书姓周,叫周男。
5. 周男的"男"是"男女"的"男",不是"南方"的"南"。
6. 周秘书对三木很客气,请他到里面的会客室里坐,给他倒水喝。
7. 周男的父母希望她像男人。
8. 周秘书说,三木汉语说得真好；三木说,周男的名字起得真好。

第二十七课　让您久等了

复习并记住下列部件的名称

工（项）　工部旁
牛（件）　牛部边
贝（贺）　贝部底

把下列各组汉字中相同的部件写在括号里

1. 设　没　（殳）
2. 签　等　（⺮）
3. 判　刚　到　（刂）
4. 贺　贵　员　（贝）

说出下列部件的名称

⺮（签）　竹部头
车（软）　车部旁
上（让）　上部边
页（项）　页部边

亅(刚)　刀部边
攵(散)　攵部边
合(给)　合部边
办(协)　办部边
欠(软)　欠部边
目(看)　目部底

把下列汉字的义符写在括号里
谈(讠)　订(讠)　散(攵)　签(竹)　判(刂)　协(办)　议(讠)

把下列各组词语中读音相同的汉字写在括号里
1. 董事　不是 (事,是)
2. 软件　看见 (件,见)
3. 等于　鲤鱼 (于,鱼)
4. 项目　向东 (项,向)
5. 项目　三木 (目,木)
6. 签订　一定 (订,定)
7. 协议　一千元 (议,一)
8. 合同　你和我 (合,和)

完成下面的句子
1. 三木先生来了。
2. 太好了!
3. 让你久等了。
4. 您散会了吗?
5. 在那里谈了几个合作项目。
6. 我刚从上海回来。
7. 谈判谈得怎么样?
8. 谈得非常好。

用竖线前后的词语做主体和述体造句
1. 王师母｜美国人
   王师母是美国人。
2. 王同｜王教授的儿子
   王同是王教授的儿子。
3. 今天｜生日
   今天是马飞的生日。
4. 马太太｜王明英
   马太太叫王明英。

5. 马飞的大儿子│马建
   马飞的大儿子叫马建。

6. 三木和林正美│韩国公司
   三木和林正美在一家韩国公司工作。

7. 我们│去过
   我们去过马飞家。

8. 马建│喜欢
   马建喜欢吃面条。

9. 二十分钟│到
   二十分钟就到。

10. 马总│开会
    马总正在开会。

根据阅读内容完成句子

1. 三木到马总的公司<u>的</u>时候,马总<u>正在</u>开会。
2. 没想<u>到</u>你来,让你久等<u>了</u>。
3. 马总听说三木去<u>上海</u>了。
4. 三木昨天刚<u>从</u>上海回来,他在那里和一家公司谈<u>了</u>几个合作项目。
5. 三木在上海谈判谈得很好,下周就要签合作协议<u>了</u>。
6. 林董事长要<u>从</u>韩国到上海签字。

第二十八课　这是互利双赢的好项目

复习并记住下列部件的名称

礻(社)　示部旁
衤(补)　衣部旁
弓(强)　弓部旁
巾(市)　巾部底
疋(定)　正部底

把下列各组汉字中相同的部件写在括号里

1. 社　视（礻）
2. 发　双（又）
3. 短　知（矢）
4. 功　项（工）

说出下列部件的名称

刂(利)　刀部边
见(视)　见部边
豆(短)　豆部边

重(董)　重部底
王(望)　王部底
取(最)　取部底
力(男)　力部底
疋(定)　正部底
廾(算)　廾部底
目(算)　目部心

把下列各组词语中读音相同的汉字写在括号里
1. 互利　　能力（利,力）
2. 希望　　西面（希,西）
3. 水平　　酒瓶（平,瓶）
4. 成功　　办公　　工作（功,公,工）
5. 市场　　重视　　教室　　不是（市,视,室,是）

完成下面的句子
1. 计算机软件市场很大。
2. 林董事长要我替他向您问好。
3. 这是个互利双赢的好项目。
4. 林董事长很重视上海的合作项目。
5. 希望他这次也来北京。
6. 他会来的。
7. 董事长夫人要来看她的女儿。

用竖线把下列句子的主体和述体隔开
1. 计算机软件｜市场很大。
2. 你们的市场开发能力｜很强。
3. 这家上海公司的软件设计水平｜不错。
4. 双方合作｜可以取长补短。
5. 我想｜一定能成功。

用双竖线把分句隔开,用单竖线分句的主体和述体隔开
1. 我们｜刚散会,‖我｜就来。
2. 这是｜大喜事,‖我｜祝贺你们!
3. 这是｜我妈给我的钱,‖我妈的钱｜比我多。
4. 中餐｜很便宜,‖下次｜请你们吃西餐。
5. 会客室｜在里面,‖您｜请里面坐。
6. 我｜路过这里,‖顺便来看看马总。
7. 我｜昨天刚从上海回来,‖在那里｜谈了几个合作项目。
8. 谈得｜非常好,‖林董事长｜下周来签协议。

根据阅读内容完成句子

1. 这家上海公司的软件设计水平很高,可是市场开发能力<u>不强</u>。
2. 马总说:双方合作可以<u>取长补短</u>,他希望双方合作<u>成功</u>。
3. 林董事长认为这是个<u>互利双赢</u>的好项目,所以非常重视。
4. 马总认为:计算机软件市场<u>很大</u>,林董事长很有<u>远见</u>。
5. 林董事长的女儿就是<u>林正美</u>。
6. 林董事长要到上海签订<u>合作协议</u>。
7. 林董事长要来北京<u>看望马总</u>。
8. 董事长夫人要来北京看她的<u>女儿</u>。

第二十九课　贵客到了

复习并记住下列部件的名称

彡(须)　彡部旁
耳(职)　耳部旁
力(加)　力部旁

把下列各组汉字中相同的部件写在括号里

1. 参　须（彡）
2. 地　场（土）
3. 职　识（只）
4. 照　绍（召）
5. 乱　话（舌）
6. 爸　吧（巴）
7. 情　忙　快（忄）

说出下列部件的名称

父(爸)　父部头
厶(参)　厶部头
非(辈)　非部头
𠂉(笑)　竹部头
包(饱)　包部边
忄(情)　心部旁
𤣩(玩)　玉部旁
元(玩)　元部边
车(辈)　车部底
力(男)　力部底
勹(句)　包部框
工(式)　工部心

附录　练习题答案

把下列汉字的义符写在括号里

1. 爸(父)
2. 感(心)
3. 情(忄)
4. 照(灬)
5. 担(扌)
6. 地(土)

完成下面的句子

1. 我先生回来说<u>了</u>,这是个好消息。
2. 他们想请您和马先生吃饭,请马建和马阳<u>也</u>参加。
3. 在北京我们是<u>主人</u>,必须由我们做东。
4. 我爸爸、妈妈这次来北京,是专门来感谢您和马先生<u>的</u>。
5. 我的实习期满<u>了</u>。
6. 马建听说你要回国,<u>还</u>担心你不回来呢。
7. 我一辈子<u>都</u>要在中国工作。
8. 马太太真会开玩笑!

用双竖线把分句隔开,用单竖线分句的主体和述体隔开

1. 我∣以前不喜欢吃面食,现在也喜欢了,‖面条、包子∣我都爱吃。
2. 三木∣说:‖"他∣没有预约,‖路过这里,顺便来看看马总。"
3. 三木∣刚从上海回来,‖他∣在那里和一家公司谈了几个合作项目,‖∣都是关于计算机软件设计的。
4. 马总∣听了很高兴,‖他说,‖这∣是大喜事,‖∣祝贺你们。
5. 马太太∣不必客气,‖我爸爸、妈妈这次来北京,∣是专门来感谢您和马先生的。
6. 这一年多以来,‖你们∣总是热情地关心我,给了我很多照顾。

根据阅读内容完成句子

1. 听说林小姐的父母要来<u>北京</u>,马家的人都非常<u>高兴</u>。
2. 林小姐对马太太说,她爸爸和妈妈要请马太太一家人<u>吃饭</u>。
3. 马太太对林小姐说,不能让林小姐的父母请客,在北京他们是<u>主人</u>,必须由他们<u>做东</u>。
4. 林小姐说,她父母这次来北京,是专门来向马太太和马先生<u>表示感谢</u>的。
5. 马太太说,他们关心和照顾林小姐是<u>应该的</u>。
6. 林小姐现在是在公司<u>实习</u>,实习期已经<u>满了</u>。
7. 林小姐回国以后还要<u>再来</u>,再来就是<u>正式职工</u>了。
8. 谈话的时候,马太太主动说起了马建和林小姐的<u>关系</u>。
9. 马建担心林小姐回国以后就<u>不回来了</u>。
10. 林小姐说,她<u>一辈子</u>都要在中国工作。
11. 马建非常<u>喜欢</u>林小姐,很希望林小姐<u>一辈子</u>都在中国工作。

第三十课　复习（六）

朗读下列各组汉字，把相同的部件写在括号里并说出它的名称

1. 安　家　实　室　客　宜　（宀）
2. 单　关　美　总　（䒑）
3. 菜　茶　英　董　（艹）
4. 老　教　（耂）
5. 六　市　京　高　离　（亠）
6. 尝　常　（⺌）
7. 有　友　（ナ）
8. 签　等　算　笑　（⺮）
9. 次　凉　（冫）
10. 软　较　辅　（车）
11. 得　很　街　（彳）
12. 功　项　（工）
13. 烧　烤　烦　（火）
14. 钟　钱　（钅）
15. 林　机　（木）
16. 体　做　候　便　件　健　位　像　优　（亻）
17. 给　结　经　绍　约　红　绿　（纟）
18. 短　知　（矢）
19. 饮　饭　饺　（饣）
20. 社　视　祝　（礻）
21. 找　打　折　接　授　（扌）
22. 汉　没　消　海　清　酒　沙　（氵）
23. 地　场　（土）
24. 情　忙　快　（忄）
25. 说　谈　语　谁　谢　该　设　计　让　认　议　（讠）
26. 鸡　欢　双　对　（又）
27. 现　理　（王）
28. 判　刚　到　利　（刂）
29. 那　哪　都　（阝）
30. 教　做　敢　散　数　（攵）
31. 开　算　（廾）
32. 蒸　点　热　（灬）
33. 会　么　去　公　（厶）
34. 定　是　（疋）
35. 句　包　（勹）
36. 道　过　远　近　这　还　迎　（辶）
37. 周　用　（冂）

根据阅读内容完成句子

1. 三木去了一次<u>上海</u>,和<u>上海</u>的一家公司谈成了几个合作项目,都是<u>关于</u>计算机软件设计的。
2. 林董事长非常重视<u>这项</u>合作,认为这是个互利双赢的好<u>项目</u>。
3. 林董事长在上海签字以后要来北京<u>看望马总</u>,董事长夫人<u>也来</u>,她要来看她的女儿林正美。
4. 马建和林正美早就成了<u>好朋友</u>,他们都非常喜欢对方。
5. 林正美到马家告诉马太太她<u>父母要来北京的消息</u>。
6. 林正美的父母这次来北京,要请马太太<u>一家人</u>吃饭,向他们表示<u>感谢</u>。
7. 林正美要和她父母一起回韩国,她回国以后<u>还要再来</u>。
8. 马太太想让林正美知道,她<u>一定</u>支持他们。